JOHN TIMPSON'S
Early Morning Book

Books by John Timpson

Today and Yesterday
(autobiography)

The Lighter Side of *Today*

JOHN TIMPSON'S

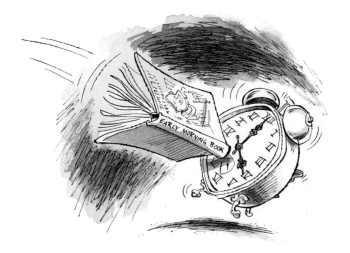

Early Morning
Book

with drawings by John Ireland

COLLINS
8 Grafton Street, London W1
1986

William Collins Sons & Co Ltd
London · Glasgow · Sydney · Auckland
Toronto · Johannesburg

BRITISH LIBRARY CATALOGUING IN PUBLICATION DATA

Timpson, John

John Timpson's early morning book.
I. Title
828'.91409   PR6070.4/

ISBN 0 00 217507 X

Photoset in Linotron Palatino by
Rowland Phototypesetting Ltd
Bury St Edmunds, Suffolk
Printed and Bound in Great Britain by
T.J. Press (Padstow) Ltd, Padstow, Cornwall

Contents

Introduction

for a great many years, in various forms, the bedside book has been
designed to distract the reader's mind from the cares and worries of
the day and lull into a pleasant, untroubled sleep – the sort of service
now provided so effectively by television. When Homer nodded, no
doubt he was reading a bedside book.

The Early Morning Book has a different purpose. It is intended to be dipped
into, not last thing at night but first thing in the morning, to ease you from
your slumbers and send you on your way, if not rejoicing then at least resigned
to your fate.

You may consider that your tightly-planned early morning schedule does
not permit the luxury of a gentle browse. There is an ingenious solution: why
not wake up a little earlier? You may be surprised how little you miss those
few minutes of sleep, and how much better you can face the day in return.

Like all profferers of good advice I would not dream of taking it myself. But
I do have an excuse. Since 1970, with one or two breaks, I have been getting
up at four in the morning to present *Today*. In doing so I have developed a
curious love – hate relationship with the early morning. I hate it when the

alarm goes. I still hate it while I dress. If I open the front door to find it foggy, or icy, or belting down with rain, I positively detest it.

But during the drive to Broadcasting House the mood softens. I picture the millions who are still a-bed and who will have to go through this process in a few hours' time, and the smugness starts to set in. When I arrive in the office and meet my haggard colleagues who have been there all night, I feel better still. By the end of the programme, if it has gone well, I can look back on the early morning with a certain affection; even more so when the cheque arrives at the end of the month.

So in tribute to a time of day which has for so long provided much of my livelihood, and a great deal of enjoyment in the process, I have delved into

other aspects of the early morning which are outside my activities on *Today*, but which I hope may serve a similar purpose – to help you start the day in a reasonably civilized frame of mind.

You may find consolation, for instance, on mornings which bode ill, in tales of famous folk over the centuries whose early mornings started well, then disastrously fell away. You may be interested in how some of the Great and the Good feel rather less than great and not too good at all in the early morning, and what they do to overcome it. The special atmosphere of the early morning has created myths and superstitions, it has inspired or appalled

the great poets, it has been a time of significant events, re-told in ways the participants may not have expected, whether it be in a Norfolk salt-marsh or a Nazarene manger. Getting up in the early morning has also, of course, been cause for alarms, from crowing cockerels to quartz clocks, and they are here too, but they should not disturb you.

I could not compile a book about the early morning without recalling some of the unlikely topics which over the last year or two have caught the eye and the ear of the nation at breakfast time; but, I promise, only a fleeting reference to the ho-ho . . .

From me – and I hope *The Early Morning Book* will help you towards it – 'A very good morning to you.'

John Timpson

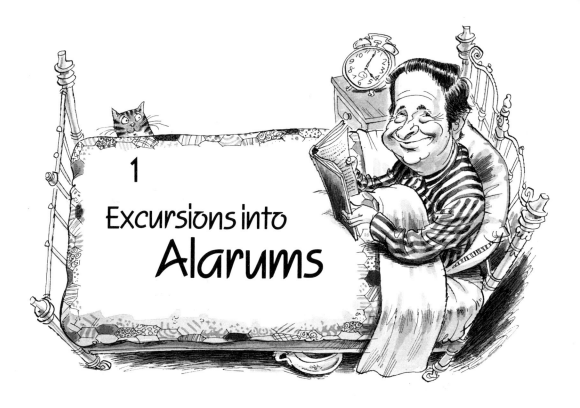

1
Excursions into
Alarums

Waking up in your own good time can be a luxurious, langorous affair. There is the first gentle twinge of consciousness, the snugness of warm sheets and blankets around you, a glimpse through half-open eyes of a ray of sunshine between the curtains, the comfortable knowledge that there is no need to rush, the world out there will wait until you are good and ready to face it.

Waking up in somebody else's time is generally quite appalling. You may try to soften the blow with a snooze button or a teasmade, but as the alarm goes or the phone rings or your spouse's elbow gets you in the ribs, the reaction must be pretty well universal: 'Why the ''@''$£!'' can't you let me sleep?' Or more simply: '@'$£!'

Waking up to order has become part of our way of life. But it was not ever thus . . .

Nobody bothered too much about timekeeping in the days of primitive man, because nobody could tell the time very accurately anyway. Either it was daylight or it wasn't, and you suited your sleeping hours and your working hours accordingly. Unless your colleagues wanted you for a dawn hunting

 10

expedition, or the chap in the next cave was beating the daylights (or the nightlights?) out of his nearest and dearest, I imagine our early forefathers woke up at whatever time they pleased. It is about the only aspect of their existence that I envy.

It was those too-clever-by-half Egyptians who were probably the start of the trouble. Somewhere around 3500 BC they invented the shadow clock and the sundial, and launched the Age of the Gnomon.

The gnomon was not an Egyptian pixie. It is the arm that sticks out and casts the shadow. On a shadow clock the time was measured by the length of the gnomon's shadow; on the sundial its shadow went round. Either way, it meant that people started worrying about the time; they have been worrying about it ever since. It is small consolation that jolly Egyptian hosts were able to confuse their guests by announcing they had a sundial with a gnomon. Or that erudite Egyptian sundial manufacturers could impress their clients by discussing the finer points of gnomonclature.

Mercifully the Egyptians, and later the Greeks and the Romans, were unable to use these devices as alarms. There was no way a revolving shadow could ring a bell, and the system would have collapsed anyway during the hours of darkness, when an alarm was most needed. You cannot see a gnomon in the gloaming.

But no sooner had they devised a way of telling the time, than they devised a way of cheating it. That famous ploy of the European Commission of 'stopping the clock' if they fail to reach agreement by a certain deadline is nothing new. Isaiah was up to that sort of caper back in the Old Testament:

'Behold,' he wrote, 'I will bring again the shadow of the degrees, which is gone down in the sundial of Ahaz, ten degrees backward. So the sun returned ten degrees, by which degrees it was gone down.'

The translators confess that 'the Hebrew of this verse is obscure', and we are not told what Ahaz had to say about his sundial being manipulated in this way, but no doubt there were similar goings-on in Egypt and elsewhere, if it was only some prankster sneaking over the garden wall and twiddling his neighbour's gnomon.

After the sundial came the sand glass and the water clock, but still nobody got around to inventing an automatic alarm. There were always trumpeters, of course, ready to wreak havoc among the slumbering soldiery as well as demolishing the odd wall, but nobody produced a mechanical substitute.

Alfred the Great may have got close to it. As well as burning cakes he also devised a system of burning candles of a specific size, which burned away in precisely four hours. Had he extended the wick so that, having burned all the wax, it then set fire to his blankets, it might well have provided the first automatic alarm system. It might even have saved those cakes. But there were still a few centuries to go before the first alarm clock came into use, and for this great boon we have to thank the Church.

Medieval monks, it seems, were a time-conscious lot. They liked to conduct their monastic offices at specific times of the day and night. In the system that prevailed up to the fourteenth century that was not too easy, because while there were twenty-four hours in the day, the hours were not all the same length. The hours of daylight were divided into twelve, and the hours of darkness into another twelve. Naturally as the seasons changed, so the lengths of the hours changed too. It has been calculated that in the summer the daylight hour could be as long as seventy-one minutes, and in the winter as short as forty-nine. At different latitudes, of course, it was different again. In places like Iceland, where in summer there is no night at all, they must have got in the most frightful muddle.

This was all too haphazard for the monks, and they started a system of canonical hours which were all the same length, so they could celebrate their offices at specific intervals. In general the nocturns were at 9 p.m., midnight

and 3 a.m., Matins came at six, then there were the daylight offices. Some of them had confusing names. You might expect Tierce, for instance, to come in the evening – 'There'll be Tierce before bedtime' – but it was actually at nine in the morning. Sext was at noon, which perhaps gave rise to the belief that making love after lunch was slightly depraved: if you did it in the afternoon you were over-Sext. The monks presumably did not worry either way. Nones was at 3 p.m., Vespers at sunset and Compline at nightfall.

Having decided the precise times they wished to pray during the night hours, somebody had to devise a way of waking them up to do it. Thus the communal alarm clock was born. Each monastery had one, an iron monster driven by weights. In one popular design it was not the hands that revolved – in fact it took a little more time to invent hands – it was the dial.

Underneath each hour on the dial was a hole, and a peg was put under the hour you wished to be roused. As the dial revolved, the peg hit a fixed arm which struck the bell. It only struck it once, so the watchman had to be a fairly light sleeper – if he missed that one stroke he might not stir until the peg came round to the arm again in another twelve hours' time. But the sequence seems to have been generally effective. The peg hit the arm, the arm rang the bell, the bell woke the watchman, the watchman woke the monks.

That was fine for the monks, who seemed to derive much satisfaction out of living as uncomfortably as possible. Unfortunately the idea caught on. The alarms got louder, and rang louder. The working day began earlier and earlier. And it was no excuse not to have an alarm clock yourself. Employers invented the knocker-up, who roamed the streets thumping on bedroom windows to make sure you made the early shift.

In the nineteenth century there was an alarm clock boom. The Germans, far too industrious as usual, were behind it. They produced the 'postman's alarm', presumably designed to ensure early deliveries. It was a thirty-hour hanging clock, weight driven, with a long pendulum and a little alarm dial in the centre of the face. They also invented the cuckoo clock, but they probably thought it too frivolous and allowed the Swiss to take all the credit.

The French, not to be outdone by their early-rising neighbours, thought of something called the 'reveille-matin', which had a pointer that was set to the figure which corresponded with the difference between the hour of setting and the hour you wanted the alarm to go off; so if you went to bed at ten and wanted to wake up at seven you set the pointer at nine. The British found all this far too complicated, and happily it never caught on here.

 13

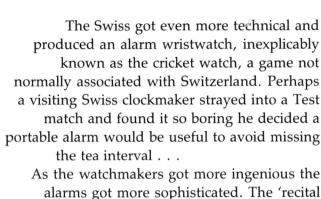

The Swiss got even more technical and produced an alarm wristwatch, inexplicably known as the cricket watch, a game not normally associated with Switzerland. Perhaps a visiting Swiss clockmaker strayed into a Test match and found it so boring he decided a portable alarm would be useful to avoid missing the tea interval . . .

As the watchmakers got more ingenious the alarms got more sophisticated. The 'recital alarm' was an eight-day clock that repeated the alarm every twenty-four hours without re-setting – which could be very inconvenient when it came to the Sunday lie-in. From springs and pendulums they moved on to electric alarms, quartz crystal alarms, and ultimately the atomic alarm clock. In recent years they have tried to devise gentler ways of rousing us. Bells can be adjusted in volume, or replaced by bleeps. The radio alarm greets you with your favourite programme. There has even been an alarm which makes no noise whatsoever, it just vibrates the pillow. Finally came 'the most exciting way of waking up since the cockerel first crowed', so the manufacturers maintained – the voice-controlled alarm clock. 'No more groping in the dark attempting to find the "off" switch,' they exulted. 'When the alarm goes off you simply tell your clock to shut up, be quiet and leave you alone! Your alarm will respond immediately, allowing you to drift back into your dreams. But sleepyheads beware – four minutes later, the alarm will re-activate until a further command is given. It will continue to do so, with a gradual increase in alarm volume, for up to forty minutes . . .'

Which sounds a great way to start the day – a forty-minute shouting match with a clock.

But not even that horological horror is going to budge you in some circumstances. W. B. Yeats summed it up:

> What were all the world's alarms
> To mighty Paris when he found
> Sleep upon a golden bed
> That first dawn in Helen's arms?

And he was late for the office again.

A challenge to early morning tea-drinkers: the tea drinking champion of the world is Martin Ternough, a London student who in 1966 drank twenty-one cups of tea in half an hour. Since we do not know the size of the cup or the temperature of the tea, this record is difficult to beat. Incidentally he was sick in the middle.

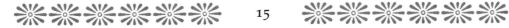 

2
Early Morning
'Today'–
and Every Day

What time do you have to get up?' Everyone asks sooner or later, and indeed I take bets with myself on how far a conversation will progress before the question is put. Not that I have any complaint; it is nice that people care. But it is not so much the time of rising that makes the job of a *Today* presenter a little different. After all, a great many shift workers get up much earlier, no doubt for much less return. It is what has to be done in the early hours that follow which provides the problems.

In my early days on the programme I used to be more than a little pompous when people observed that I rose no earlier than the average baker, or postman, or market porter. 'But the average baker,' I pointed out loftily, 'does not have to grasp the latest report of the OECD at 5.30 in the morning. The average postman does not have to interview a particularly devious union leader before breakfast. The average market porter does not have to devise a jolly introduction to a zoologist who encourages polar bears to mate by showing them blue films. And having done that, none of them has to try to be civil to five million people . . .'

These days I hope I would put it a little more humbly, but basically the same argument applies. Now, back to the question.

The alarm goes at ten to four. In the days when I stood in for Jack de Manio, back in the 1960s, the programme did not start until seven, it contained many repeated items and very few 'live' interviews, so a 5.30 call gave ample time for preparation. It is a measure of the programme's increased complexity (or of my own flagging faculties) that when it was moved forward to 6.45 a.m. in the 1970s I used to get up at 4.30, and now it is a quarter of an hour earlier I have moved the alarm forward by another forty minutes.

The alarm itself has mercifully become gentler over the years. There used to be the appalling din of the traditional clock with the little hammer on top bashing away at the bells on each side. Then for years I relied on 'Little Ben', which offered the alternative of a loud or a soft bell. It was supposed to be permanently set on 'soft', but occasionally the switch was accidentally moved and the racket was all the worse for its unexpectedness. Now, thank heaven, there is a more melodious range of equipment available, but even in this age of high technology there still seems no effective device for rousing one occupant of a double bed without disturbing the other. 'Sleep somewhere else' is the obvious solution, but there is a limit to how unsocial one can allow unsocial hours to be.

I have never slept through an alarm and the alarm has never failed to go off. Nevertheless I still set a second clock to go off five minutes later. In theory I should sleep more securely because of this double protection. In fact I am generally awake before either of them goes off anyway.

So, a murmured farewell to the huddled figure under the bedclothes, an uncertain flounder to the bedroom door, and into the blinding hundred-watt dazzle of the bathroom. And there before me is the familiar assemblage – trousers draped over the towel rail, shirt and tie on the linen basket, shoes and socks under the washbasin, wristwatch and wallet on the windowsill, jacket hanging up behind the door. The positioning is crucial. Drape the jacket on the towel rail and I would be trying to stuff my feet up the sleeves. Put the socks on the basket and I would wrap one around my neck. Move the shoes away from the basin and I would never find them at all. Most people find it helpful to have a routine in the early morning; without mine I would be blundering around the bathroom till lunch.

In spite of it I have still slipped up. My bathroom, like a computer, can only supply what it has first been supplied with. There have been some nasty moments in the early morning when I find I have forgotten to put a belt in the trousers, or a comb in

the jacket pocket, or cufflinks in the shirt. Sometimes a button comes off, a shoelace breaks, a zip refuses to zip. On one disastrous morning the seat of my trousers split. Generally the problem can only be rectified by stumbling around the darkened bedroom in search of a substitute, which is not too popular a procedure and one I try to avoid. Which is why on that particular morning I kept my jacket on throughout the programme, and addressed the nation in a permanent draught.

The routine for leaving the house is equally precise. There is a creaky stair to circumnavigate, a briefcase to be retrieved from the hall table, the front door to be silently wrestled with (it is inclined to stick on damp mornings), and the gate to be opened. Then the moment of truth as the key is turned in the ignition . . .

I have been offered a taxi to the office, but I have seen the problems that taxis have in conveying bodies to Broadcasting House in the early morning, even from Central London. Certainly the Knowledge that taxi-drivers are so proud of does not extend beyond the Green Belt. So I have always driven myself to work, and by the grace of God and Henry Ford I have not missed a programme yet.

The route has changed vastly over the years. It is sobering to recall that when I joined the BBC the first stretch of the M1 was not even completed. Indeed I reported the opening ceremony at what is now Newport Pagnell Service Area, and watched Harold Watkinson, then Minister of Transport, wandering unscathed in the fast lane. Now I can drive along the new M25 to the almost-as-new M40, and instead of a succession of lights and roundabouts along the old Oxford Road it is mostly underpasses and flyovers until the Marylebone Road. In the rush hour that means that instead of a series of moderate traffic jams you can now enjoy just one really monumental one; but at 4 a.m. it makes for very fast motoring indeed.

I sometimes regret the loss of those interruptions on the journey. They not only served to keep me awake, they also provided a little vicarious social intercourse at a time of day which normally offers only solitude. As I waited at each traffic light there would probably be a familiar vehicle in the next lane. There was a rogue newspaper van which always took off before the lights changed, and a battered fishmonger's van, presumably en route to Billings-gate, which reeked so powerfully it could always be identified before it actually pulled up. And there was a game little Morris Minor which chugged along purposefully in the slow lane, oblivious of the long-distance lorries roaring

past it, and which had some difficulty winding itself up when the lights turned to green; I often feared it would still be quivering there impotently when they went back to red again.

On one deserted stretch of dual carriageway, far from any habitation, there always used to be a sturdy figure striding towards apparently open country, flat cap pulled over the eyes and umbrella at the slope. He waved genially to us as we all drove by, and I dipped my lights and other drivers dipped theirs, in comradely salutation. I often speculated what he was doing there. Where did he start from, and where was he going? Was it just an early morning constitutional, or some sort of vigilante patrol? Or was it the shade of some long-deceased local, who used to stroll through the peaceful fields to commune with the rabbits, in the days when communing took precedence over commuting? It is some years since I last saw him but occasionally, as I pass that spot, I am tempted to dip my lights again in his memory . . .

For most of the year the drive to work is dark and unappealing. In winter, with snow and ice and fog, it can be downright unpleasant. But for about six weeks at the height of summer it is actually getting light at that hour of the early morning, and I can gloat over the slumbering citizenry, missing the growing glow in the sky and the first rays of the sun as the dawn comes up like thunder out of the City beyond Westway.

It takes me 28½ minutes to drive to Broadcasting House, which provides an invaluable period for the mind to get into gear. It also provides the World Service news; and the careful enunciation of my newsreading colleagues at Bush House, designed to be audible around the world through all manner of jamming and atmospherics, is ideal for imparting information to a listener only a few miles away whose brain is still running on two cylinders. Incidentally I always relish the apocalyptic finale to the bulletin: 'That is the end-of-the-world news.'

Thanks to the World Service I have occasionally arrived at the office with more up-to-date knowledge of the state of the world than my colleagues, who have had no time to listen and have yet to check the tapes. But normally it is I who have to catch up, and that starts as soon as I get in the door.

The original *Today* office at 4.30 in the morning was not an edifying sight. For six days a week it was occupied around the clock; as one shift ended, another began, and there was little chance to clear up in between. The desks became submerged in books and papers, there were half-cleared plates and half-empty cups, litter overflowed on to the floor. The little fridge in the corner, intended to preserve the milk for the coffee, contained nameless horrors, unfinished snacks now in advanced decay, gruesome liquids congealing in the bottom. There was once a coffee machine, but

 20

it was rarely scoured and gradually choked to death. The kettles which replaced it burned out regularly. The carpet below was a stained and sodden sponge. Small creatures occasionally browsed among the debris.

That was the office that served us for over a decade and it had literally a life all its own. At its best it was scruffy, at its worst it was squalid, and to me it was an old friend. Now we are in elegant new quarters, where the carpets are still pristine, the files are actually filed, the desks are naked and shining, there are no facetious cuttings on the walls and the fridge and kettle have been banished to a separate room. It is clean and workman like, and quite soul-less. But give it a year . . .

The arrival routine is as exact and unchanging as those that have gone before. A grunted good-morning to whoever happens to be around, briefcase on the desk, jacket on the hook, and a glance at the 'runners and riders' board for the first indication of what is to come. The board lists the 'live' interviewees due to appear that morning. It can sometimes be an impressive catalogue of household names, but sometimes the Great and the Good have to mingle with the Grafters and the Ghastly. It can be people suddenly in the public eye, or people seldom

 21

out of it; people we have never heard of, people who are all too familiar. They may be on a telephone in Tanzania or in a studio in Stoke-on-Trent. They may have arranged to come into the *Today* studio ('NC NC' are the simplest: 'No Call, No Car'), they may not even know yet they are on the programme. They all have one common attribute. For one reason or another – and sometimes, I confess, that reason escapes me – they are in the news.

Having scanned the list and absorbed the initial shock, it is easier to cope with the key document that forms the basis of the programme, the provisional running order. It has been known to limp rather than run, but it has been prepared with varying degrees of loving care by the overnight team, who took over from the day team at 6 o'clock the previous evening and will remain on duty until the programme is over. Compiling the order, as they not in-frequently remind me, is a complex and delicate procedure. So many factors must be borne in mind: giving the right prominence to the right items, balancing the serious with the eccentric, avoiding a succession of telephoned interviews or of items by the same reporter, ensuring the presenters have a fair proportion of interviews themselves. The whole concoction of bulletins and summaries, interviews and features, sports spots and 'God-spots', travel flashes and weather forecasts, are timed more or less to the second. And if a new story breaks, or a line goes down, or a guest fails to appear, the result of all that labour can be scrapped in mid-programme and we start all over again.

With the running order come the 'prospects'. These were drawn up by the day team in time for the 6 p.m. handover the night before. They summarize, sometimes most entertainingly, what has been set up for the programme in advance. Many news stories are predictable – reports to be published, meetings to be held, speeches to be made, opening ceremonies, close-down demonstrations, new books coming out, old stars saying farewell. The day team provides the pre-recorded items, books guests, and suggests – sometimes somewhat optimistically – what further action might be pursued.

The night team – generally a night editor, a couple of producers, a reporter and, most indispensable of all, two secretaries – deals with the overnight events (mostly from overseas countries which are still enjoying daylight), gives a final polish to the recorded items, ensures there is material for the cues and briefings for the 'live' interviews, and actually produces the programme. Many writers from newspapers and magazines have joined them on their vigil and produced accounts of what they do. I would not presume to add another. But one day the full story of the *Today* night shift will be written by one of

their own number, preferably after leaving the programme. And that account I must not miss . . .

Five o'clock, and the Entry of the Other Gladiator. Brian Redhead appears, humming. The humming is an integral feature of his arrival, and I have never been quite sure whether he hums because he feels cheerful or because he likes to give that impression, or just to let us all know he has arrived. But a humless morning would be a disturbing experience, like a sunrise without any birdsong.

However, sunrise is still a long way except at the height of the summer. Before then we have to study the briefings, drawing attention in the nicest possible way to their failings – no wonder we are referred to on occasions as the Brothers Grimm. We plan as best we can the pattern of our interviews, we catch up on the papers, occasionally we may actually exchange a word. Then at 5.30 more or less precisely we put the first sheet of paper into the typewriter. The raw material is there, we have to adapt it to what we like to think is our own style of presentation. In the case of straight news stories, there may only be the odd word or phrase that needs adjusting. With the lighter items it is gratifying to concoct something a little more individual. Often the right phrase does not come to mind until we are actually on the air, and it is the great merit of a live programme that we can alter and embroider as we go along. All too often, alas, it does not come at all.

A few minutes before 6.30 we gather up our scripts and cuttings and our third or fourth cups of coffee and head for the studio. The newsreader is in the next chair, the production team is behind the window, the closing phrases of 'Prayer for the Day' are on the loudspeaker. A brief exchange of greetings, a final check on which of us reads the headlines and who says good-morning, then the loudspeaker is switched off and a voice in the headphones announces, 'It's 6.30 – time for *Today*.'

The rest you know.

3
Early Morning
Omens

The early morning is the time of day which lends itself not only to the Muse and the faintly amusing, but also the awesome, the mystical, the supernatural. It is a great time for auguring. It can augur well or augur ill, or just generally augur.

Perhaps it is the mist rising in the half-light, the first rays of the sun coming over the horizon, the crispness and glitter of the frost, or just the vaguely out-of-focus feeling that can follow too heavy a celebration the night before. Whatever it is, the early morning mists can lead to early morning myths; many an early morning omen has emerged from the early morning gloaming.

The Druids may well have started it. The old wives were not far behind. These are some of the tales they tell, a dollop of saws with your breakfast.

For the British the weather is the first consideration, and what Briton has not been brought up on the theory 'Red sky at night, shepherd's delight; red sky in the morning, shepherd's warning'? Actually it is based on sound meteorological thinking. In Britain at any rate the prevailing winds come from the west. So do the rainclouds. On a clear night the red glow of the sun sinking in the west will reflect off the clouds to the east – in other words the

clouds which have already passed, so the night should be fine. But in the morning the glow from the sun rising in the east will reflect off the clouds approaching from the west, so rain is on the way. Whether the shepherds worked all that out, or whether they just looked in the next field to see if the cows were sitting or standing – who knows?

It is difficult to find any such scientific backing for that other traditional early morning forecast, 'Rain at seven means fine by eleven,' perhaps because just as many people quote it as 'Sunshine at seven, rain by eleven.' One way it means we can never have a day of continuous sunshine, the other (a ludicrous proposition in Britain) we can never have a day of continuous rain.

Perhaps the American version is more accurate. 'When the dew is on the grass, rain will never come to pass. When grass is dry at morning light, look for rain before the night.' America being such a vast place, with such a vast range of weather, it must be true somewhere.

The early morning dew can not only act as a weather guide, its cosmetic properties seem quite remarkable. If you rise early enough, particularly on May the First, rubbing dew on your face will ensure a lovely complexion for the next full year. Better still, though you may find it chillier, rush out on the morning of St Bride's Day, February the First, and give your whole body the dew treatment – a few rolls in the grass would be the speediest method.

YOU'RE LISTENING TO THE TODAY PROGRAMME..... AND NOW FOR THE WEATHER FORECAST

You will guarantee yourself an unblemished skin, and a few odd looks from the neighbours.

The merits of getting up with the lark are widely advertised. Better still, get up just after the lark, pinch three of its eggs (assuming you have no misgivings about this sort of activity) and be sure to eat them before the church bells ring on a Sunday morning. This is supposed to ensure you have a sweet singing voice. It will also, alas, greatly reduce the lark population if practised too widely.

Having acquired this talent, do not be tempted to make use of it in your early morning bath. Not only can it be tedious for the neighbours, no matter how many lark's eggs you may have consumed, it can also bring you bad luck. A proverb circulating in many European countries maintains that he who sings before breakfast will cry before night. Similarly, avoid any early morning guffaws. 'Better the last smile than the first laughter,' they do say. But as someone who occasionally tries to coax a breakfast time titter from the listening public, I prefer to regard that as just a European version of 'He who laughs last, laughs longest,' without any great early morning significance.

Finally, ponder on this. It comes from Herbert's *Collection*:

'In the morning, mountains. In the evening, fountains.'

If you can make any sense of that, I am sure Herbert would love to know. Personally, I think he was having us on.

The old Norse word for dawn was dagr. Hence the early morning greeting: 'Is this a dagr I see before me.'

4
Early Mornings with the Famous

*g*etting up in the morning can be just as tedious for top politicians and show business celebrities as it is for us, and they can feel just as dreadful. Few of them, like few of us, can claim as boldly as Douglas Fairbanks: 'I think I am rather good-tempered in the morning.' But then if you are in your seventies and you are still called Junior, you have to be good-tempered. More likely we have mornings like Simon Groom of *Blue Peter*, who confesses: 'There are some mornings when I get up with a sinking feeling, and I can't eat my breakfast because of the day ahead.' In this case the day ahead can involve climbing a factory chimney or canoeing over a waterfall to entertain his young viewers, but for us it can look just as bad if we are merely due to visit the dentist.

Many of the famous cope the same way that we do, by following an automatic routine through the teacups and the toothbrushes. Cliff Richard, for instance, switches on the radio, cleans his teeth, shaves, exercises and showers. 'It is a dead set pattern and there is no way I would change it,' he is reported to have said. 'There would be nothing wrong with shaving first or showering first and then cleaning the teeth, but you do get into that sort of pattern.'

Some do terribly intelligent things in the early morning, like Mrs Thatcher, who studies her government papers, and Susan Hampshire, who learns lines for two hours. Others do not do terribly intelligent things. Barry Norman, for example, jogs.

So the famous adopt a variety of techniques in the hope that they will continue to be famous for another day.

The Newsaholics

Perhaps by definition famous people are interested in news. They like to know what people are saying about them and what they are reported to have said about other people. They want to see what has been happening in the world which may have some impact on them and, in the case of politicians, what has been happening on which they may have had some impact. All the leading members of the Royal Family are into newspapers and news programmes in the early morning (the Queen, as you would imagine, reads *The Times* over her boiled egg and toast; she also studies *Sporting Life*) while the Prime Minister, we are told, listens to *Today* between 7 and 8 a.m., a period noticeable for the surfeit of hopeful Conservative backbenchers jockeying for a place on the programme.

Most of her fellow politicians follow her example. In the David Owen household, for example, the alarm goes at 6.50 and he listens to the programme from 7 a.m. onwards – assuming, of course, that he is not appearing on it himself. Typical of MPs of all parties is Dr Oonagh McDonald, Labour member for Thurrock, who takes her radio around the house with her in the early morning, listening in particular to the Parliamentary report, 'essential listening when the House is sitting, and even better when they quote *me*'.

Among the Lords a much earlier start is made by Lord (Gerry) Fitt, whose years of harassment in Northern Ireland have made him a sporadic sleeper even though he now lives in England. ('Sometimes I feel like going out and throwing things at my front door in the early morning, to make myself feel at home.') He finds it difficult to know precisely when his morning starts. He listens to the World Service off and on throughout the night, again concentrating on the news and the Parliamentary reports.

Former politicians do not get out of the habit, and they can start early too. T. Dan Smith, former Labour leader of Newcastle City Council, starts the

day with the 5.30 news and listens through the farming news and the first part of *Today* before getting up. Then his first action is to pick up *The Times* – not to read it but to check his Portfolio card. The Bishop of Durham *does* read *The Times* – first the home news, then the page opposite the leader page, and finally the letters. He reckons he can complete the operation in seven and a half minutes, excluding the sports pages which he never bothers with. He takes the *Guardian* too, but does not always get around to it, and who can blame him.

David Dimbleby starts with the *Daily Mail* and the *Mirror* because, unlike *The Times* and the *Financial Times*, they are the right size to read in the bath. Writer Alan Bleasdale, creator of *Boys from the Black Stuff*, always buys the *Mail* – 'Dip your fingers in Dettol before and after, but I have to know what *they* are up to.' He also has the *Guardian* and the *Mirror*, presumably to know what *we* are up to. On Sundays he divides his attention very fairly between the *Sunday Times* and the *News of the World*, the *Observer* and the *People*.

Having listed some of *Today*'s followers, it is only fair to mention a distinguished renegade. Robert Robinson, one of its former presenters, still wakes up at five o'clock but these days goes back to sleep until eight or nine. 'I never listen to the radio in the morning. This will sound like very fancy footwork indeed, but before I did *Today* I had never heard it and since I stopped doing it I haven't listened to it. I can't say it doesn't smite my ear by accident, all I say is I get up too late for it. I listen to the radio at other times, but not in the morning.'

The author Rumer Godden would be relieved to hear that. She once said she was the only person she knew who did not turn on the radio in the morning. 'I like absolute silence, which is difficult to find in this modern world.'

At the other extreme are people like the advertising whizz-kid Tim Bell, who devised the pin-striped flour men and the Conservative election campaigns. He is one of the few famous folk who admits to watching breakfast television. He switches it on at 7 a.m. and only forsakes it in the shower, when he cannot see the pictures because of the water running down the glass. He reads all the papers as well. 'Sunday is a real treat,' he reckons, 'the papers are much bigger and children's programmes on TV are much better.'

The Exercisers

The joggers have not yet taken over the world but the famous do often favour a little exercise in the early morning. Some do it because of their particular line of business. Sebastian Coe, for instance, trains until breakfast time, which may not sound excessive but then he doesn't have breakfast until eleven. Doreen Wells, who as a prima ballerina has to be as fit as any athlete, does ai-ki-do exercises for up to half an hour in her garage, now converted into a dojo, or practice room. She took up ai-ki-do when a bad foot prevented her doing her usual dance exercises. 'They are wonderful exercises for physical and mental wellbeing. I have found ballet much easier ever since starting them.'

Soldiers must keep fit too, even top soldiers, which is why military men like Major General Peter de la Billiere, when he was commander of the British forces in the Falklands, went for a twenty-minute run every morning before breakfast. 'I have done it all my life. I don't make it too difficult; if I did it would be easy to find an excuse not to do it!'

Among the world's presidents, nobody has really solved the mystery of Ronald Reagan's eternal middle age, but early morning exercising must have something to do with it, even if it is only toning up the cheek muscles to get that smile going. On the other hand President Amin Gemayel of Lebanon is only forty-three but with all his problems he could be forgiven for looking

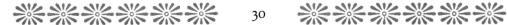

twice that. 'Each morning when I wake up at 7 a.m. I always feel as though I haven't had enough sleep,' the poor chap confesses. So to get himself going he does fifteen minutes' exercise before breakfast – concentrating, one imagines, on ducking and weaving.

In show business it helps to look fit too, though early morning exercise will not necessarily guarantee it. My good friend Barry Norman, for instance, runs 3½ miles every morning and still cannot eliminate those splendid bags under the eyes. Maybe he should really work at it like Larry Hagman of *Dallas*, who has pictures taken of himself on his exercise machine. He spends an hour each morning running and exercising. His house is built around a giant jacuzzi and he has notices in the rooms saying 'No Smoking'. As a result, instead of looking fifty-three, he only looks about fifty.

Virginia Wood, comedienne and composer, gets rather better results with a forty-length swim every morning. She started it when she had to lose weight for a role she was playing and keeps it up even when she is on tour, if a pool is handy. The good-humoured Douglas Fairbanks Jr, when he is at home in Florida, will swim before breakfast and walk three or four miles, and is doubtless still smiling at the end of it. He has fewer problems than Ms Wood finding a pool when he travels, because there is one at his London club. 'Laps are boring,' he observed, 'so I try to amuse

myself with mental games like thinking how many choruses of how many Gershwin or Cole Porter songs it will take to get through.'

The same devotion to early morning exercise is not shared (as you can imagine) by Frankie Howerd, who confesses that he only does exercises in spasms. 'Each spasm will last a week or two, then I tell myself, "That's enough."' He is a little vague about the form each spasm takes. 'I don't jog or mess about with weights or go to the gym. It's more sort of muscular tone-up stuff.'

Peter Cook has much the same idea: 'My beauty routine is a mixture of aerobics, isotonics, isometrics and a little bit of yoga. To the observer it would look as if I was merely lifting a cup of coffee to my lips and lighting a cigarette. But it's through mental control that you are in fact exercising every muscle in your body and cleaning out the brain of all the toxins that can gather while asleep . . .'

But let us not mock the early morning exerciser. Take the ever-youthful Cliff Richard. 'If I don't look my age I feel grateful for that, but first thing in the morning I think I do,' he says. Then he does fifteen minutes' exercise between shaving and showering, and he is a teenager again. Would that we could all work the same miracle.

The Up-and-Abouts

Susan Hampshire, not only the star of so many plays and films but an author in her own right, gets up early by choice. 'If I am writing then I get up at five

and work for three hours, because that is the only time I can get without the phone ringing. Or I might do a couple of hours in the middle of the night, getting up from two until four and then going back to bed.'

Rosie Swale is someone else you may not immediately associate with writing. She made the headlines when she sailed around the world with her husband and had two children. She made news again when she spent four years with a sex-change seaman. 'Sex,' she was quoted as saying, 'is distinctly easier on land than at sea, with the marmalade sliding off the shelf towards you.' Perhaps this action-packed career encouraged her to make an early start when she took up writing.

'I wake up restlessly and look at my watch. It is only four o'clock – a beautiful frosty night, the moon and stars are out and the sky is clear . . . I put a tape of classical music on because it helps me to write, and I try to do two new chapters of my book. It is not made any easier because my typewriter still has arthritis in its keys after coming across the Atlantic with me. It's a brilliant feeling when my writing goes right – the greatest adrenalin booster in the world and better than any orgasm.' (I can appreciate the arthritic typewriter; I am not so sure about the orgasm.)

It must be added that a lot of people get up early besides writers. Postmen for instance. And Prime Ministers. Take Aneerood Jugnauth, known to his friends, I imagine, as the Aneroid Juggernaut but actually Prime Minister of Mauritius. He is also Minister of Defence, Minister of Internal Security, Minister of Information, Minister of External Communications and Minister of Reform Institutions. No wonder he has to get up early – six o'clock, to be exact.

'It is not too difficult because in the tropics light comes early, and the mynahs in the mango trees make certain you do not go back to sleep.' Mrs Thatcher is also an early riser of course, but she never allowed any 'mynahs' to disturb *her*.

The Lie-Abeds

As you would expect from the late hours they mostly work, show business folk in the main are late risers. Fairly typical, I imagine, is the routine of Ruth Madoc, who does a lot of stage work as well as running Maplin's Holiday Camp, and admits to lying in bed until 9.30 after an evening show. This sort

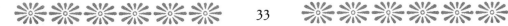

of thing has its effect on a spouse. Alan Jay Lerner, lyric writer of *My Fair Lady* and *Gigi*, used to be up at six, 'bursting with ideas'. He did much of his creative work in the early morning. Then he married the singer and actress Liz Robertson, who needed to sleep late to catch up after her late-night performances. So now he lies in, too, until eleven.

Novelist Anthony Powell gets up at 7.30 but 'doesn't enormously hurry about getting down', which means breakfast at a quarter to nine. On a good morning he is at his typewriter by 9.15, on a rather bad one at 9.45. Fellow writer Alan Bleasdale gets up at 8.30, 'too late to be any help in the house'.

Even the energetic Russians like a lie-in given the chance. Galina Vishnevskaya, former star of the Bolshoi Opera now living in France and America, never sets an alarm clock because the only mechanical objects she trusts are kettles and electric irons. And Rudolf Nureyev never breakfasts before nine. 'Thank God I can at least afford to have someone to cook, do my laundry and clean my apartment.' The maid brings his breakfast.

One final example of a late-riser, but her reasons are quite different. Cynthia Payne never gets up before ten. 'I am not much good for anything in the morning. Mornings always depress me. I come alive about four.' Cynthia Payne? Better remembered as Madame Cyn, who achieved national notoriety with her sex parties in Streatham, issuing 'luncheon vouchers' to ageing businessmen for a package deal of sex, films, drinks and poached eggs on toast – but not for breakfast.

Fasters and Breakfasters

Surprisingly to those who do eat breakfast, a great many people do not. A survey in America showed that the number who ate nothing before going to work had increased by a third in five years to nearly twelve million, and no doubt the same applies over here. Certainly there are many famous folk who forego any forage before noon.

So we find the Prince and Princess of Wales nibbling at a piece of wholemeal toast with their coffee (Prince Charles has a scrape of honey as a treat); Mrs Thatcher has black coffee without sugar and a glass of orange juice; the Earl of Bradford just has orange juice 'though I sometimes get seduced into breakfast at weekends'; Clive Jenkins moistens up for another day's hard talking with apple juice and tea; Debbie Moore of the Pineapple Dance Studios keeps off the fruit, she just has wholewheat bread and Earl Grey tea; Susan Hampshire takes toast and China tea, standing up in the kitchen; Douglas Fairbanks Jr beams over a piece of dry toast, fruit juice and tea; Barry Norman eats nothing at all – 'the thought just turns my stomach'.

Happily not all the famous have allowed the Great British Breakfast to dwindle so drastically. Sebastian Coe, after his first three-hour workout of the day, cooks himself bacon and eggs with apple juice and tea or coffee. Doreen Wells, after all those ai-ki-do exercises, fills up with two eggs, potatoes, fried bread and bacon, and sometimes tomatoes. Only when in a hurry does she cut down to two raw eggs in milk with sugar and brandy. Ruth Madoc has egg and bacon with mushrooms and grilled tomatoes. T. Dan Smith sometimes adds to that grill some fried banana – 'I introduced that to make it a bit more Parisienne than Tyneside.'

That takes us to the more exotic tables of breakfasters like Virginia Wood, who starts the day with a fistful of vitamins and mashed banana on toast. Meanwhile in Mauritius Aneerood Jugnauth is treating himself to coconut pancakes, and in Libya President Gaddafi is savouring a glass of camel's milk. It all sounds more exciting than roughing it with the roughage, but many people now just dip into the bran tub for breakfast. Galina Vishnevskaya has bran crackers with margarine; Larry Hagman has bran and yoghurt; Alan

Bleasdale has a bran biscuit with his Weetabix. In the Age of the Fibre Diet even the famous merely brandish a bran dish for breakfast.

So here is something to make their mouth water, the breakfast which has been enjoyed for so many years by the famous and the infamous, the notable and the notorious, ministers of state and ministers of religion, academics and alcoholics – the *Today* breakfast. In the 1960s it was served on a table in a hospitality room; now it is served on a trolley in the office, but the ingredients have hardly changed.

First course, a packet of cereal to be emptied into a cardboard plate which is a miniature replica of the hat worn by Olivier in *The Entertainer*. It can be moistened with milk from a plastic container. Granulated sugar is no longer supplied, so if you require it sweetened you have to pulverize a sugar lump with the heel of the shoe. It used to be done more elegantly with repeated blows from a spoon; then the spoons became plastic too, and they succumbed before the sugar.

Second course, a choice of toast, piled high to ensure maximum moisture content, or pre-packed croissants, baked to last. All washed down with either tea or coffee, and contrary to popular belief they are easily distinguishable: there are different coloured tops on the Thermos flasks . . .

The Meditators

Many famous people start the day with meditation and prayer. Not so many famous people will admit it. Those who do range from Malcolm Muggeridge to Colonel Gaddafi. Mr Muggeridge told an *Any Questions?* audience: 'This is going to sound rather priggish but it's the truth.

'Now that I am an octogenarian and soon to depart from this world, I wake up in the morning with my equally long-lived wife beside me and we say our prayers. I have found this a rather marvellous way of starting the day because you are going to relate what happens in it to these eternal considerations. We read from the Book of Common Prayer and a passage from the Bible, and introduce some prayers of our own, and on that basis start the day.'

The writer Rumer Godden, now widowed a second time, lets out her two Pekinese when she wakes, makes some tea, and goes back to bed. 'That is where I do all my reading and thinking and a bit of meditation. I discovered

Catholicism when I came back to England from India and now I keep the offices going during the day, exactly as if I were a nun.'

And Colonel Gaddafi? 'Each day I consider that I have been dead, and that I have just awakened and am about to start a new life. And the first thing I start with is my prayers. I have to pray and thank God for the day that is beginning. I live from day to day, so I also ask for forgiveness for any transgressions that I have committed.'

The Archbishop of Canterbury could hardly have put it better.

The Individualists

If you have not developed a satisfactory process for getting the day under way, some of these thoughts from the famous may help you. For a gentle start, why not try the Rudolf Nureyev system. He gets his brain into gear by cogitating over a crucial question: should he have a bath first and tea after, or tea first and a bath after? Either way, by the time he has decided, he has woken himself up.

Virginia Wood takes a more energetic line. 'I hurl myself out of bed at seven every morning. I don't hang about because if I do I only start worrying – will I be able to get the wardrobe door open, will my clothes have shrunk mysteriously in the night, will the car start, will the baths be on fire when I get to the Leisure Centre in Kendal?'

Victoria Gillick, she of the ten children and the Cause, starts the day on military lines. 'I wake at half-past seven and go down and put a huge pot of porridge on the stove. My husband helps, and at twenty to eight I go round and wake all the children. The older ones make their beds and when the porridge is on the table I clang the big handbell in the hall and down they all come.'

 37

If your day always starts painfully, so does that of Tommy Smith, captain of Liverpool in the 1970s (he headed the winning goal for them in the 1977 European Cup Final), now director of the Cavern Club of former Beatles fame. One of his many footballing injuries was a kick from a Sporting Lisbon player (it was the club that was Sporting, not the player) which chipped off the side of his kneecap and all the ligaments attached to it. His first action when he wakes now is to take a painkiller with a glass of lemonade. 'I should say "cheers" to that chap from Lisbon I suppose. But maybe someone's got *his* knee by now.'

Anne Mallalieu, first woman president of the Cambridge Union, now a barrister, starts the day at her farmhouse home by milking her cow. But her rural life has its gruesome side in the early morning. 'I check to see how many livestock have survived the night, and take a spade to those which haven't. During the lambing season that is a frequently used tool. Then I go in to what coffee I can face, to recover from the shock and horror that has met me outside.'

Better perhaps to cling to a more imaginative approach. Peter Cook reports that he rises at 6.30 a.m. and calls Tokyo, because most of his current speculation is in the yen. Then he calls the manager of his jojoba farm in northern California, which he hopes is a good long-term speculation, though last year it only produced three ounces of pure jojoba oil from its 5000 acres. Then he breakfasts in the bathroom with a statue of Dorothy Squires, and collects his thoughts while being shaved by his Personal Daintiness people. Then at eight o'clock he has got Roxanne, who is his bodyguard and a qualified masseuse. She is very expert and often it is all over in five minutes . . .

The key to all that, I suspect, is in the jojoba, pronounced ho-ho-ba.

5
That Early Morning in Bethlehem

✝he story of the first Christmas morning has been told and acted so often in kindergartens and Sunday schools, yet no two versions are ever quite the same. The basic ingredients are there: the Angel appearing to Mary, the shepherds watching their flocks, the three wise men from Orient far, Joseph and Mary turned away at the inn, the Babe lying in the manger. Yet somehow a six-year-old can manage to provide a totally different interpretation of a familiar role, or adjust the story to suit present-day conceptions. A small child's adaptation of that early morning in Bethlehem, and the events that led up to it and followed it, can be quite disarming. These incidents involving casts and classrooms at Christmastide are all vouched for as authentic by the listeners who sent them in to *Today*.

The Rebellious Innkeeper

A small boy was bitterly disappointed at not being cast as Joseph in the school Nativity play. He was given the minor role of the innkeeper instead – and throughout the weeks of rehearsal he brooded on how he could avenge himself on his successful rival.

 39

Came the day of the performance. Joseph and Mary made their entrance and knocked on the door of the inn. The innkeeper opened it a fraction, and eyed them coldly.

'Can you offer us board and lodging for the night?' pleaded Joseph,

impeccably following the script. 'My wife is soon to have a baby.' They stood back, awaiting the expected rebuff.

But the innkeeper had not pondered all those weeks for nothing. To the

confusion of the producer and the delight of the audience he flung the door wide, beamed genially at the couple and cried hospitably: 'Come in, come in. You are very welcome. You shall have the best room in the hotel.'

There was a pause. Then the youthful Joseph displayed the resource and initiative which perhaps got him the part in the first place. With great presence of mind he said to Mary: 'Hold on – I'll take a look inside first.' He peered ostentatiously past the innkeeper, shook his head firmly and announced: 'I'm not taking my wife into a place like that. Come on, Mary, we'll sleep in the stable.'

The plot was back on course . . .

And The Exonerated Innkeeper

A Sunday School teacher was telling a group of four- and five-year-olds the story of that Christmas morning and explaining that Jesus was born in a stable because (regardless of what that mutinous innkeeper may have said) there really was no room at the inn.

A worldly-wise little Yorkshire lad at the back of the class was heard to murmur to his neighbour: 'I blame Joseph. He should have booked.!

Shepherds Strike Back

All was going smoothly at the Nativity play, but the scene involving the shepherds was dragging on a bit. The discussion over what they had or had not seen in the way of itinerant angels may have been engrossing for the ones who were doing all the talking, but a couple of walk-on shepherds at the back,

whose role was to lean on their crooks looking attentive, were getting very bored indeed. They had no lines to speak, and didn't really believe in angels anyway.

It came to the point where they could stand the inaction no longer. In the middle of the discussion they suddenly pointed their crooks towards the audience, shouted 'Bang! Bang! Bang!' and ruthlessly 'machine-gunned' the entire hall.

What's In a Name?

Such disconcerting moments can occur quite unintentionally. At a primary school Nativity play in Cheshire it happened even earlier in the performance. The first scene had passed without incident. Mary was told by the Angel who was blessed by God and would be giving birth to His holy child.

Then came Scene Two. Enter Mary and Joseph, chatting.

Mary: 'I met this fairy in the garden. He said I'm going to have a baby.'

Joseph: 'Great! What are you going to call it?'

Mary: (totally forgets next line. Then, after thinking hard) 'Colin.'

Exit Mary stage right, followed by a puzzled Joseph muttering: 'Colin Christ?'

Any Odd Jobs in Heaven?

The story of the Annunciation also caused a problem for a cub scout group in the East End of London. A Sister told them the story, ending with Mary's reply to the Angel: 'Behold the handmaid of the Lord.'

She asked one of the cubs to retell the story in his own words. He went through it very accurately until he came to the last lines, when somehow he managed to replace Mary by Joseph. In his version it was Joseph who answered the Angel, with a slight variation on the original.

'Behold,' said Joseph, 'behold the handyman of the Lord.'

Flights of Fancy

The Flight into Egypt has conjured up some strange images among the very young. A teacher at one primary school told her class the story of the Angel

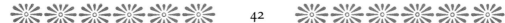 

appearing to Joseph in a dream and saying: 'Take the young child and his mother, and flee into Egypt.' The children were asked to illustrate the story.

One small boy drew Joseph leading the donkey on which Mary was riding. He had the donkey's bridle in one hand and in the other he carried a walking stick with a large black dot on top.

'What is that meant to be?' asked the teacher, pointing to the dot.

'That's the flea,' he explained.

Another child in another class but depicting the same subject, came up with a more modernistic approach. For the flight into Egypt he actually drew an aeroplane. There were four figures discernible inside.

The teacher decided to make the best of it. 'Very nice,' she said. 'I can see Joseph and Mary and Jesus – but who is the one in front?'

The little lad looked at her proudly. 'That's Pontius the Pilot,' he said.

Food for Thought

Biblical names can all too readily become confused in the young mind with similar names or phrases of the present day. For them the Christmas characters can be full of pitfalls, just like Pontius the Pilot.

The mother of a little girl decided that with Christmas approaching it would be appropriate to tell her the Nativity story at bedtime. Her daughter listened with great attention.

A few nights later, after tucking her up, her mother asked her which story she would like to hear this time. The response was immediate. 'Please, Mummy, do tell the story of the little cheeses in the straw.'

Another family were choosing their favourite Christmas cards from the dozens they had received. The youngest daughter had no doubts at all. 'I know which one I like best,' she said, 'it's the one with the MacDonald and Child.'

6

The Early Morning Muse

The Great Romantics have ever been inspired by the early morning. 'Prose can paint evening and moonlight, but poets are needed to sing the dawn,' said George Meredith (conveniently), and the poets duly responded, whether it was Wordsworth proclaiming that earth had not anything to show more fair, or Tennyson urging Maud to take a turn in the garden now that the black bat, night, had flown. They have discussed in great detail what dawn looks like, what happens at it, how we should greet it, occasionally why we should ignore it. 'There is no solemnity so deep, to a right-thinking creature, as that of dawn,' pontificated Ruskin. So his literary colleagues took a deep breath, and concentrated . . .

The first decision they had to make was its colour. This sort of thing can be a grey area, and a lot of them left it that way – just plain grey. John Masefield, itching to go down to the seas again, was looking forward to 'a grey mist on the sea's face and a grey dawn breaking'. Julia Crawford tried to rouse Kathleen Mavourneen with the uninviting information 'the grey dawn is breaking'. Joseph Addison was even gloomier about the prospects: 'The dawn

is overcast, the morning lowers, and heavily in clouds brings on the day.'
And on the road to Mandalay, you will recall, it was less promising still.

Milton couldn't make up his mind about the right tint of dawn. 'Morning
fair came forth with pilgrim steps in amice grey,' he wrote. But amice is
recorded as the cloth worn by clerics round their necks, traditionally white,
so either they had very grubby necks or Milton was aiming at a sort of
off-white. Elsewhere he gives another clue. 'The *dappled* dawn doth rise,' he
wrote. So – white *and* grey?

Others preferred a more glittery approach. Thomas Hood relished the vision of a young lady who stood breast-high amid the corn, clasp'd by the golden light of morn. A. E. Housman visualized 'the silver sail of dawn'. And who is this, moving into the precious metal and jewellery market? 'Now morn, her rosy steps in th'eastern clime advancing, sowed the earth with orient pearl.' It's Milton, hedging his bets.

Note that for good measure he threw in 'rosy' as well, thus linking up with another shade of literary opinion. Shelley recalled 'when the red morning's brightening', Alfred Noyes wrote of the 'red dawn in Sherwood', Cecil Frances Alexander enjoyed 'the roseate hues of early dawn'. Samuel Butler put it less elegantly but came to the same conclusion: 'Like a lobster boil'd, the morn from black to red began to turn.' Robert Browning took a similar culinary line: 'O'er night's brim, day boils at last.'

Shakespeare preferred his morn a little browner, 'in russet mantle clad'. And the last word goes to Milton, still side-stepping through the spectrum, with a morn that 'purples' the east.

One way or another, in one colour or another, the happy morn has arrived. Time for Christians to awake and salute it. Early in the morning, after all, our song shall rise to Thee. But some of our sonneteers are none too keen. 'Oh sleep, it is a gentle thing, beloved from pole to pole,' wrote Coleridge, reluctant to let it go. 'Blessings on him who invented sleep,' agreed Cervantes, 'the mantle that covers all human thoughts.' And Robert Bridges makes no bones about it. 'As night is withdrawn,' he advises, 'dream, while the innumerable choir of day welcome the dawn.'

But there is always the energetic one, the early rising essayist who has to be first with the muse. And guess who is pulling off the covers: 'Awake, arise, or be for ever fall'n!' Yes, Milton is already up and about. So is Longfellow, warbling over the wigwams: 'Onaway! Awake, beloved!'

Edward Fitzgerald goes about it rather more wordily. 'Awake! for Morning in the Bowl of Night has flung the Stone that puts the Stars to Flight.' (If he tried that today he might have something flung back at him.) Robert Bridges is a little more coaxing. 'Awake, the land is scattered with light, and see, Uncanopied sleep is flying from field and tree.' And Sir William Davenant was a right little charmer. 'Awake, awake, the morn will never rise, till she can dress her beauty at your eyes.'

Personally I go for this plea from Thomas Moore, directed at the more mature of us. 'Then awake! the heavens look bright, my dear; 'Tis never too

late for delight, my dear; And the best of all ways To lengthen our days Is to steal a few hours from the night, my dear!' How much more civilized than Robert Herrick's abrupt approach: 'Get up, get up for shame, the blooming morn . . . has come.'

The response, as you will already have gathered, is not always too kindly. Robert Burns is particularly firm. 'Up in the morning's no' for me, up in the morning early.' But Isaac Watts knew his sort. ' 'Tis the voice of the sluggard; I heard him complain, "you have wak'd me too soon, I must slumber again". As the door on its hinges, so he on his bed, Turns his sides and his shoulders and his heavy head.'

Mr Watts, you may remember, was all for little birds in their nests agreeing, and little busy bees improving the shining hour. No wonder he took a poor view of late risers. And how he would have approved the unbelievably elegant response of John Donne when his good lady nudged him awake. 'Dear love, for nothing less than thee Would I have broke this happy dream . . . thou wak'd'st me wisely; yet My dream thou brok'st not, but continued'st it.' Try that tomorrow morning, instead of 'Where's the tea?'

If you are a poet, of course, these things come naturally first thing in the morning. Hilaire Belloc, for instance, had no sooner surfaced than he was declaiming to the neighbours: 'The moon on the one hand, the dawn on the other: The moon is my sister, the dawn is my brother. The moon on my left and the dawn on my right. My brother, good morning: my sister, goodnight.' And off to the bathroom.

Having been roused, what next? Not everybody can start the day as enthusiastically as Robert Browning. 'The year's at the spring And day's at the morn; Morning's at seven; The hillside's dew-pearled; The lark's on the wing; The snail's on the thorn: (Well, it had to rhyme with morn) God's in his Heaven, All's right with the world!' Of course Milton will have a try: 'Sweet is the breath of morn, her rising sweet.' But to be on the safe side, he says much the same about the evening as well. 'Sweet the coming on Of grateful evening mild, then silent night.' A man for all seasons, was Milton.

Back to the early morning. A variety of experiences can await you. You may hear a maid sing in the valley below, accompanied by the horn of the hunter, heard on the hill. You may spot Kipling's gunner, sniffing the morning cool, as he walks in his old brown gaiters along o' his old brown mule. If you are a drunken sailor, of course, your experience may be rather less pleasant.

If it is your wedding morn you should have no problem: 'Joyful hour we

 47

give thee greeting,' as they sang in *The Mikado*. But what about the morning after? 'It doesn't much signify whom one marries,' wrote a sour Samuel Rogers, 'for one is sure to find next morning that it was someone else.' Sir Walter Scott confirmed that 'with the morning cool repentance came'; and Elizabeth Barrett Browning had much the same message: '"Yes" I answered you last night, "No" this morning sir, I say. Colours seen by candlelight will not look the same by day.'

So how do you get over this early morning depression? Charles Dickens was all for a bit of jogging, or its Victorian equivalent. 'What better time for driving, riding, walking, moving through the air by any means, than a fresh frosty morning, when hope runs cheerily through the veins with the brisk blood and tingles in the frame from head to foot?'

After the jog, a quick shower – Dr Johnson recommends you wash yourself with 'oriental scrupulosity'. William Collins would prefer you to wash your hair too – 'Bathe thy breathing tresses, meekest Eve.' Then join Izaak Walton and the Compleat Angler for 'A good, honest, wholesome, hungry breakfast'; though be warned by A. P. Herbert, 'The critical period in matrimony is breakfast-time.'

It is not very likely, I fear, that we can return to Tennyson's days of King Arthur 'when every morning brought a noble chance, and every chance brought out a noble knight'. The best we can hope for is to go along with Longfellow's village blacksmith, 'Each morning sees some task begin, Each evening sees it close; Something attempted, something done, Has earned a night's repose.'

But before you set off on the working day and a whole new range of literary allusions, pause a moment to envy the early morning experience of Lord Byron. 'I awoke one morning,' he wrote quite simply, 'and found myself famous.' It is the difference between ploughing through *The Oxford Dictionary of Quotations*, and actually appearing in it!

> Early morning prayer for civil servants: *O Lord, grant that this day we come to no decisions, neither run into any kind of responsibility, but that all our doings may be ordered to establish new departments, for ever and ever,*
>
> *Amen.*

 48

7

Early Mornings That
Started Well,
Then Fell Away

You know the feeling.

You wake up knowing that this is going to be a good day. Maybe it's your birthday, or the start of your Spanish holiday, or you've planned to spend a peaceful day in the sunshine at Lord's. There's a rosy glow to the morning; you may even hum a little.

And of course nobody remembers your birthday . . . the Spanish air traffic controllers go on strike . . . and at Lord's it rains all day.

As a small consolation, here are a dozen far more drastic examples of how a promising start to the day can end very unpromisingly indeed, sometimes with quite remarkable repercussions.

Sir Cloudesley Shovell

On a foggy morning in 1707 Admiral Sir Cloudesley Shovell awoke on board his ship, homeward bound off the Scillies. He was doubtless looking forward to digging into some home cooking with the rest of the Shovells, back in Norfolk. Indeed, perhaps he was rejoicing once again that, with such a down-to-earth surname, his parents had had the imagination to give him as

 49

piquant a forename as Cloudesley – though Piquant Shovell might have been more fun.

Anyway, there he was off the Scillies, on his way home from the wars in triumph, and only a few miles from port. But the story goes that he had a violent quarrel that morning with his pilot, decided to hang him from the yardarm for insubordination, and promptly ran aground. The story is difficult to verify since the ship went down with all hands – all except Sir Cloudesley himself, for whom the day could still have improved again. He struggled ashore and was discovered by a local housewife. Far from giving him succour, however, she took a fancy to his emerald ring and struck him a blow to obtain it such that his already weakened system could not withstand, and he forthwith expired. She buried him nearby and it was thirty years later, on her deathbed, that she finally confessed to the crime.

The body was exhumed and Sir Cloudesley went to his final resting place in Westminster Abbey, at the end of a very long day.

William Henry Harrison

On a bitterly cold morning in Washington, in January 1841, William Henry Harrison woke up with the pleasant knowledge that today was to be the summit of his career. He was already a military hero – years earlier he had defeated the Indians at the Battle of Tippecanoe and the British at the Battle of the Thames (the one on the Canadian border). His election campaign managers had turned him into a folk hero – they depicted 'Old Tippecanoe' as a simple frontier farmer, with a log

cabin and a barrel of cider as his campaign symbols, even though he actually lived in a sixteen-room mansion in Ohio.

Now he was a political hero, with an overwhelming majority in the electoral college of 234 votes to 60, the first Whig victory in the party's history. And this morning he was to be inaugurated as President of the United States.

But it was indeed bitterly cold, and it got no warmer. And William Henry Harrison, at 68, was no longer a young man.

In spite of the weather, the open-air ceremony went ahead as planned. There were the crowds, the parades, the march-past, the in auguration address, all the formal speeches. William Henry Harrison got colder and colder. By the end of the proceedings he was snuffly and shivery. The cold he had caught developed into pneumonia. The new president took to his bed; within a month he was dead.

FOOTNOTE: On a bitterly cold morning in Washington, in January 1985, Ronald Reagan woke up with the pleasant knowledge that he too was to be inaugurated that morning. President Reagan was even older than President Harrison – and a lot wiser. He postponed the parade and had his inauguration indoors . . .

Capt. Nolan, 15th Hussars

On the morning of 18 October 1854 a certain Captain Nolan, a dashing young officer in the 15th Hussars and aide-de-camp to Sir Richard Airey, was hoping to win more laurels in what had been for him a very successful war. He had acquitted himself creditably in a number of engagements, his only fault perhaps being over-impetuosity, and impatience with those who did not share it, including some of his superior officers. Now another battle was under way and he was chafing to be a part of it.

He was no doubt delighted, therefore, when ordered to take a message from the Commander-in-Chief's safe vantage point on the hills above the battleground to one of the commanders in the field. It was his chance to get in the thick of it again. He duly delivered the message to the commander, Lord Lucan, one of those he considered by nature over-cautious; indeed he had nicknamed him 'Lord Look-on'.

The message read: 'Lord Raglan wishes the cavalry to advance rapidly to

 51

the front, follow
the enemy and try to
prevent the enemy carrying
away the guns . . .'
Lord Lucan, it seemed, queried the order.
'Attack, sir? Attack what? What guns, sir?'
Nolan had no time for such prevarication. 'There, my lord,
is your enemy,' he cried. 'There are your guns.'
But in his impatience he pointed, not at the redoubts
Lord Raglan meant, where the Russians were trying to carry away
some captured guns and might well have been easily overrun,
but in a totally different direction, towards some strongly-emplaced

Russian batteries, up a valley overlooked by more guns on the heights on either side. The order was passed to Lord Cardigan, who also queried it without success. In the charge of the Light Brigade which followed, of a total strength of 673, 113 died, 134 were wounded, and 475 horses were killed, ending the Brigade's existence as a fighting force. Captain Nolan, impetuous to the end, rode at the forefront. He was killed by the first enemy shell.

Kevin Moran

18 May 1985 looked like being a memorable day for twenty-seven-year-old Kevin Moran. He was going to play for Manchester United in the final of the FA Cup. He awoke knowing he was lucky to have a place in the team: Graeme Hogg should have been playing, but he was out through injury. Even so, the football writers thought he was a good choice. 'A brave defender, great experience, likes to get forward for set pieces, capable of snatching a goal,' said the *Mail*. 'With his goal-scoring forays he might even be a matchwinner,' said the *Guardian*, and added: 'Hard, craggy and almost too courageous in going for dangerous balls.'

Alas, too true.

In the 78th minute, with the score still nil-nil, Kevin Moran's great day fell dramatically away. He hurled himself not at the ball but at Peter Reid, as he was breaking through for Everton with only the 'keeper to beat. Reid turned a somersault, referee Peter Willis blew his whistle, and Moran made football history. He became the first player to be sent off in an FA Cup Final. And when he climbed the steps with the rest of his team to collect his medal, he came down again empty-handed.

The story has a not entirely unhappy ending. Galvanised by the referee's

 53

decision, United's remaining ten men scored the goal which won them the Cup. Five days later, the FA Council decided that Moran could have his medal after all.

Professor Landrey Slade

Professor Landrey Slade, assistant president of the American University in Beirut, had had a harrowing twenty-four hours. He had been on board a Jordanian Boeing 727 which was hi-jacked as it flew out of Lebanon on 12 June 1985. The six gunmen on board were demanding the evacuation of all armed Palestinians from the Beirut camps, and the planeload of passengers spent many tense hours being shuttled between Lebanon, Cyprus, Tunisia and Sicily before the gunmen ordered the plane back to Beirut. At last they were allowed to leave the plane before it was blown up on the tarmac.

After all that, next morning the world looked rather better to Professor Slade. He was heading out of Beirut again on his delayed holiday, this time on a plane of Middle East Airlines. He was trying to put the memories of yesterday's hi-jack behind him.

Approaching Larnaca Airport in Cyprus a Palestinian holding a hand-grenade rushed into the first-class cabin shouting: 'This is a hi-jack . . .'

The professor's response is not recorded. We do know that the stewardess, with considerable aplomb, greeted the Palestinian with the words 'Ahlan wa Sahlan,' which you might reasonably assume to mean 'What, again?' It actually means 'Welcome.'

The hi-jacker and his grenade took control of the aircraft, and it emerged that he was having his own back for the hi-jack the previous day. This time, would the passengers be allowed to escape?

Happily, the professor's day did not fall away completely. When the plane landed at Larnaca they were all allowed off the plane to safety. The Palestinian finally gave himself up and was put on a flight to Amman. Professor Slade has also flown since. It seems unlikely that he particularly enjoys it.

Francis Bacon

On a crisp morning in 1626 Francis Bacon (who of course enjoyed crispness) decided it was a good day for a ride in his carriage around his estate at

Gorhambury. As he set out, he must have been feeling that in spite of past vicissitudes, life was now treating him well. He had held illustrious government office, then had come disgrace and dismissal. But, like many others who have suffered compulsory early redundancy, he had started a second career. He took up writing; and considering that much of it was in Latin, he had done remarkably well.

Admittedly, even his English works were not aimed at the popular market. Few of us might be gripped by a title like *Apophthegms New and Old*, even if we could pronounce it. And his latest, catchier title, *The New Atlantis*, was not an attempt at science fiction but a treatise of political philosophy. So sales were not exactly booming, and he was still some £22,000 in debt.

No matter. The intellectuals lionised him, and his reputation as a philosopher was made. Now, as he drove off in his carriage, he was thinking about another aspect of his activities, as an amateur scientist. He had some interesting theories he wished to pursue, in particular the preservative properties of intense cold.

Francis Bacon had always preached the virtue of caution, of 'long and close intercourse with experiments and particulars'. Alas, he failed to display sufficient caution himself. He stopped his carriage and lingered in the biting cold, gathering snow with which he intended to stuff a goose or a chicken, to see if it would keep the bird from spoiling. It must be small consolation to him that his theory was quite correct, and the refrigeration industry has cause to be grateful for it. Bacon caught a chill while he gathered the snow; the bird may have been preserved, but Bacon died a few days later.

Alexander Romanov

13 March 1881 looked like being a good day for Alexander Romanov, Czar of all the Russias, when he woke up in his Winter Palace. Plenty of snow about, of course, and a biting wind, but he was due to take a significant step forward on one of his favourite projects – reforming the constitution to give the people a greater say in their own affairs. He was going to sign a document which would allow elected representatives to join the Central Council of State. It would only be in an advisory capacity, but it was a start.

There were a few Czar-type chores to do first. From the Winter Palace he drove to inspect a military parade. Like most military parades, it went very

55

smoothly. Alexander took the salute, congratulated the men, and set off again in his carriage to the signing ceremony at his palace.

The first bomb that was lobbed at the carriage left him uninjured. It looked as though this attempt to assassinate him was going to fail like the two previous ones. A bomb in the state dining-room had gone off before his arrival, and a mine intended to derail the Imperial train had failed to go off at all.

This time, however, his luck finally ran out. As he enquired about the injuries to his escort and watched a young anarchist being arrested, a second bomb was thrown. Czar Alexander II returned to the Winter Palace lying mortally wounded in the back of an open sleigh. He died from his wounds a few hours later.

The document was never signed, the reforms were never made. And thus, in due course of time, came the Revolution.

Mayor Wilson Goode

Mayor Wilson Goode, black Mayor of Philadelphia, woke up on 12 May 1985, remembering that today he was going to take a step which should prove popular with his black constituents, who lived in one of the poorer and more congested suburbs of the city. They had been complaining for weeks about the behaviour of a group of back-to-nature radicals called Move, who shunned such modern contrivances as dustbins and lavatories, and kept their house in the heart of this crowded neighbourhood in a state of appalling squalor. Today the Mayor was coming to the rescue. It was going to be a Goode day.

With his authority the city police moved in. After five hours of violent exchanges involving water-cannon, tear gas and rifle fire, Move still hadn't been moved. Mayor Goode gave his approval to the dropping of a stun-bomb on the house.

It was the same sort of stun-bomb that was used in the Iranian Embassy siege in London, but it produced rather different results. Instead of disabling the beseiged group with non-lethal shock waves, it started a fire that swept through the suburb and burned sixty houses to the ground. Damage was estimated at more than five million dollars.

Five bodies were found in the house. The rest of the group got away.

 56

240120 Cpl. William Wood, 4th Gordon Highlanders

The British Army's training and reinforcement camp at Etaples in northern France during the First World War had a regime reported to be so sickeningly brutal that men pleaded to be sent to the front line to face the enemy instead. The instructors and military policemen were renowned for their sadism; there was constant bullying and humiliation for new recruits and battle veterans alike. It was a recipe for rebellion.

On the morning of 9 September 1917, Corporal William Wood of the Gordon Highlanders, 'resting' from the front line, awoke looking forward to the comparative idleness of a Sunday in Etaples Camp. Reveille at 7 a.m. instead of five, only five periods of parades and training in the Bull Ring before noon, even a film show at the camp cinema.

He left the barbed-wire compound where the Scots were billeted, his tunic unbuttoned in the heat, and on the road he met a WAAC, a girl he knew from Aberdeen. They stopped for a chat. For Corporal Wood, the day had started well.

Then, according to eyewitnesses, a military policeman reprimanded him for the offence of talking to a WAAC, and for being improperly dressed. He ordered him to move on. There was shoving and pushing, a punch was thrown, and the military policeman drew his revolver and shot William Wood through the head.

The news of Wood's death swept round the camp. For the battle-weary Highlanders, already resentful and rebellious over their treatment, it was the last straw. The Etaples Mutiny was on. Thousands of Scots, New Zealanders, Australians and English united to overcome the police and the officers and take over the camp. And in six days their demands were granted: the camp police were transferred, the Bull Ring was closed, regulations were relaxed, and the commandant was sacked. Order was restored.

Within weeks, many of those men were killed at Passchendaele. They were buried with William Wood in the military cemetery at Etaples. But according to one commentator, 'they had successfully defied the worst brutalities of an old-style militarism which, if it had been allowed to persist, could well have meant Britain and her Allies losing the War.'

Prince Rozhestrensky

When he awoke on board his battleship on a foggy morning in the autumn of 1904, the Russian Imperial Admiral Prince Rozhestrensky must have been feeling rather pleased with himself. He was leading the Baltic Fleet halfway round the world to take on the Japanese. Two days earlier he had had a splendid ceremonial send-off from Riga. The Czar himself had toured the ships and blessed them. Now he was ready for action.

It came sooner than he expected. Through the fog came a signal from the supply ship *Kamchatka*. She was being pursued by torpedo boats! The Imperial Admiral did not hesitate: he gave the order to open fire. Being more of a prince than an admiral, it apparently did not occur to him that the Japanese were unlikely to have torpedo boats roaming the North Sea in the neighbourhood of the Dogger Bank.

The entire fleet kept up an intensive barrage on the 'torpedo boats' for twenty minutes. Only when the fog cleared and they were celebrating a notable victory did they discover they had sunk sixty trawlers and three mother ships from the Hull fishing fleet, while they had been peacefully fishing for cod.

Miraculously only two British seamen were killed and six wounded, but it very nearly started an Anglo-Russian war. The repercussions were disastrous enough for

Prince Rozhestrensky. Britain closed all its ports to him and he was forced to take the long route to the Far East around Africa instead of through the Suez Canal. Fever broke out, coal ran short, men deserted and finally mutinied. When the prince eventually confronted the Japanese fleet, his own was virtually wiped out. Twenty-three ships were sunk, nearly five thousand Russian sailors died. Russia lost Port Arthur, and the war.

Dickinson H. Bishop

Dickinson H. Bishop, heir to the Round Oak Stove Company of Michigan, and his bride of five months, Helen, woke up in their first-class cabin looking forward to another carefree day's cruising to round off their prolonged honeymoon. They had been all over Europe and parts of North Africa. Now they were sailing back to the States and their new two-hundred-thousand-dollar home. It was 14 April 1912.

The day did indeed pass most amiably. In the evening they returned to their cabin and Mrs Bishop went to bed, while Dick Bishop stayed awake reading. At twenty minutes to twelve, as the day was ending, there was a slight jar and a grinding noise, not enough to wake Helen Bishop but enough to cause Dick to abandon his book and go on deck. Other passengers were wandering about, but there seemed no great cause for alarm.

Still uneasy, he woke his wife and together they went on deck again. There they met a steward, Alfred Crawford, who cheerfully reassured them. 'You go back downstairs,' he told them. 'There is nothing to be afraid of. We have only struck a little piece of ice and passed it.'

The 'little piece of ice' was actually some seventy feet high. It had damaged the ship irrevocably. Less than three hours later the *Titanic* sank, and 1522 people drowned or froze to death.

Dick and Helen Bishop were among the survivors. They got away in a lifeboat and were picked up and taken to New York. But even for the Bishops the story has an unhappy ending. Back home, rumours spread that Dick Bishop had dressed in women's clothes to be allowed into the lifeboat. Their marriage suffered, they were divorced a few years later. Dick Bishop remarried – and his ex-wife Helen died the same day.

 59

Richard Coeur-de-Lion

On the morning of 24 March 1199 King Richard of England, as usual, was not in England. His Crusading days over, he was now spending much of his time retrieving those parts of his empire in France which King Philip had over-run while he was away. The year before he had routed Philip at Gisors, personally unhorsing three French knights with a single lance, to the delight of his tame troubadours! 'He charged upon them like a hungry lion upon his prey' – and all that. Since then he had signed a truce with Philip. The empire had struck back.

But this morning he had a little local difficulty. A peasant within his territory had found some buried treasure and taken it to his lord, Achard of Chalus. Richard decided the treasure should be his, and besieged Achard's modest castle. The garrison is said to have consisted of only fifteen men, so poorly armed that one of them, a crossbowman, had to make do with a fryingpan for a shield.

Achard offered to surrender if his men were spared. The Lionheart, in one of his less benevolent moods, declined. It was after all a small nut to crack. And this March morning looked a promising time to take the castle, hang the garrison, remove the treasure and perhaps be home for tea. So he rode casually within bowshot of the battlements to select the weakest point for the assault. Whereupon the soldier with the fryingpan put it to one side, aimed his crossbow and deposited an iron bolt in the monarch's left shoulder.

Richard made light of it. He had after all survived worse than this in his Saladin Days. He told his general to take the castle, which he speedily did, and rode back to camp, where awaited him an incompetent surgeon, gangrene, and eleven days later a painful death.

Before he died, he performed one final act of chivalry. He ordered the pardon of the man who shot him, he of the fryingpan. Alas, the fryingpan was only exchanged for the fire. Without the king's knowledge the crossbowman was flayed alive and hanged. His day too fell away . . .

8
Early Mornings in Norfolk

'Oh yes, Norfolk,' people will say, nodding knowledgeably. 'It's very flat in Norfolk.' And the shrewd Norfolkman will probably agree, because he is thus discouraging another foreigner from invading his county. These days one can detect breaks in the ranks. There is a campaign to turn the tortuous road to Norwich into a dual carriageway; they have even opened a tourist information office in Fakenham. But in the main it is a matter of no great regret that the M11 disintegrates before it reaches the county border, and the Eastern Region of British Railways maintains the fine tradition of the London and North Eastern Railway – combined with the North Sea, it successfully cuts off East Anglia from the rest of the nation.

Actually Norfolk is no flatter than most of Cambridgeshire and Bedfordshire. Perhaps the fens in the west and parts of Broadland in the east have given that impression to casual visitors. But head northwards through mid-Norfolk ('High Norfolk' they like to call it, with a touch of whimsy) and in the triangle marked out by Dereham, Swaffham and Fakenham (my friends will hate me for this) you will find rolling hills and wooded streams and unspoilt villages clustered around some of the finest medieval churches in the country. Flat? Try it on a bike . . .

 61

You may also of course find a fair amount of feudalism, a certain lack of amenities, and the sort of biting wind that can only be experienced if there is nothing between you and the Arctic except the North Sea. But it is worth all that to enjoy the special quality of life that Norfolk can offer, not least in the early morning.

Thirty years ago, when I worked for the local paper there, I contributed a series of weekly articles called 'From the Heart of Norfolk', an immigrant's impressions of rural life in East Anglia, viewed from a cottage where the sanitary system was a metal bucket down the garden, the water was handpumped from a well, and to do the washing you first lit a fire under the copper.

Now I have a foothold in Norfolk again, in another old cottage with rather more amenities but the same distinctive ambience, part of a community and a lifestyle which has hardly changed over the centuries, and over the last thirty years not at all. Those articles could have been written yesterday. Three of them were about rather special early mornings which I suppose illustrate some of the favourite leisure pursuits of the average Norfolkman: shooting duck, catching fish, and becoming a parent . . .

The Duck Shoot

Four o'clock in the morning on Cley salt marshes is generally very much the same as four o'clock in the morning anywhere else in Norfolk – dark, deserted, and probably pretty nippy. But this was 12 August, and scattered along the banks of the marsh were the first duck-shooters of the season.

The genuine duck-shooter spends the night on location, camping out in a suitably camouflaged tent so the ducks have got used to having you around by the time it is light enough for you to shoot them. This singularly dismal summer, however, had discouraged all but the most fanatical from such a drastic procedure.

So the party which had me in tow reached Cley about 4 a.m. We must have looked a motley lot. Leading us was a character I always think of as the Jovial Enthusiast, because he was, even at four in the morning. His wife was half his size but twice as enthusiastic; I suppose she had to be. Then came their cousin on leave from the Navy; their two young sons; their fourteen-year-old daughter; two French girls on an exchange visit, who seemed a trifle dazed; and a solemn retriever, who had seen it all before.

 62

When one has risen at 3 a.m. and driven for miles through a sleeping countryside, it is rather disappointing to find anybody else actually awake. One loses that self-satisfied glow which is the only consolation of the enforced early riser. But the cars parked by the Cley beach road and the occasional glow of a cigarette further along the bank proved that this duck-shooting business was a bigger attraction than I had suspected.

We took up our position in the grass on a vacant stretch of bank. The Jovial Enthusiast and his cousin tinkered with their guns, the children, trained from birth to cope with such situations, curled up under a blanket and went to sleep. The French girls continued to look dazed. I found myself wrestling fiercely but silently with a now strangely over excited retriever.

'Which way,' I asked between rounds, 'will the ducks come?'

'Duck!' said the Jovial Enthusiast. So I did.

I had pressed my face into the damp grass for some seconds before I realized he was merely drawing attention to my faux pas. There is no such word as 'ducks', of course, to a duck-shooter. I did not pursue the question.

So there we crouched. And as I crouched I might have pondered on the people who could have occupied that spot on previous August the Twelfths. People like Sir Cloudesley Shovell, scourge of the Barbary corsairs, who may well have ridden over from his home at Cockthorpe to bring down a duck for lunch. Or his contemporary, Captain Grieve, who fought under him at Tripoli and those tomb stands in Cley churchyard. Or the de Warrennes or the Erpinghams or the de la Poles, whose arms adorn the church itself.

I might well have pondered on such matters. Actually, I was far too busy grappling with the wretched dog.

The light gradually improved. A noise like a train running through an endless station indicated the waves breaking on the beach a quarter of a mile away. Otherwise everything was still. Then, from far away over the marshes, came the hoarse cry of a bird.

The cousin gripped his gun, the children woke up, the retriever and I called a truce and we both looked expectantly at the Jovial Enthusiast. 'Heron,' he said. We all subsided.

Half an hour later the sky over the top of the bank was turning red, then yellow. A seagull flew over to have a look at us and flew away again, squawking derisively. I could hardly blame it. Then the dawn really broke. The soft glow in the east became stronger and the marsh, with its little pools and lush grass, could be seen clearly. Away behind us the tower of Blakeney

Church stood against the clouds, and in the foreground we could see the cottages clustered around Cley windmill. A plover was calling in the distance and the sea still rumbled on the beach. It was a scene to delight Peter Scott and his fellows. Only one thing was needed to complete the picture. There were no duck.

There were still no duck by half-past five, when the sun appeared briefly to tantalize us before disappearing behind cloud for the rest of the day. Along the bank there were signs of restlessness.

To our left a gaunt figure stood erect against the skyline, shotgun at the slope, vaguely reminiscent of a palace guardsman except for the old billycock pulled over his eyes. In the other direction little groups started wandering around in the lee of the bank, all clad in gumboots, old macintoshes and several layers of sweaters, standard wear for a Norfolk morning. There was also another dog, which proved too much for our retriever. To my relief it left us for the rest of the morning.

By this time even the Jovial Enthusiast looked discouraged. He joined a council of war being held by the leading lights on the bank. One of them maintained he had seen two duck an hour before, but they were out of range. They had all heard the sound of a shot over Blakeney way. But that, apparently, was all.

Inevitably it began to rain. The children decided they were hungry – an announcement which brought the two French girls out of their daze for the first time. The shoot, we decided, was over.

It was while we were toasting bread over an oilstove that the situation suddenly changed. Away in the distance we saw a group of birds, a score or so, heading in our direction. Immediately we were on the alert. Toast was discarded, guns were seized, the children were pushed behind cars.

The Jovial Enthusiast studied the oncoming flight, then straightened up wearily as the birds wheeled above us. 'Curlew,' he grunted, and resumed his toast. Guns were lowered as they made a final circuit and disappeared over the bank, still flying in a tightly bunched covey.

If that is the word. At the time I thought of a much better one.

The Early Worm

We stood silently at the lake's edge, the Angler, the Angler's Mate and me. A steady drizzle of rain was falling, our gumboots were gripped in six inches

of glutinous ooze. A fishing rod pointed mockingly at the gloomy sky. A church clock struck five o'clock – in the morning.

It had been a chance remark that sent me out into another early Norfolk morning. Someone mentioned that the Angler regularly rose before dawn to put in a few hours' fishing before going to the office. 'There's a story for you,' said somebody else. 'But you'd never get up in time.'

I reminded them indignantly of my article about the duck-shoot. Nobody had read it. Nobody had met anybody else who had read it. I suspect nobody believed it had ever been written – or if it had, I had invented it. There was no alternative; that night I set the alarm for 4.30.

'Have a nice time,' muttered the Little Woman as I reeled out of bed, while the rain pattered against the darkened windows. 'Bring me back a big one.' She was asleep again in a moment. I snarled silently.

Down in the kitchen the Pooch stirred on his chair, looked at the clock (a remarkable dog, the Pooch) and eyed me in amazement. 'One sound and I'll take you with me,' I snapped. He shuddered, lowered his head, and gave an unconvincing snore.

The cup of tea tasted foul. The biscuits stuck in my throat. My stomach, not expecting to report for duty for another four hours, protested noisily. I felt like death.

The battery of the car, of course, was down. I cranked wearily in the darkness, with visions of a quarter-mile push to the nearest downward slope. By the time the engine fired the sweat was dripping out of the sleeves of my raincoat and I hated the entire world.

I was still getting my breath back when I drew up at the lakeside. The Angler, already ensconced behind his rod, beamed at me through the dusk. 'Wondered whether you'd make it,' he said. I shrugged nonchalantly. 'Of course I've made it,' I said. 'No trouble at all . . .'

I joined him at the water's edge. The net beside him was conspicuously empty. 'No luck yet?' I asked, trying not to sound too mocking. 'Plenty of time,' he said cheerfully. 'Only been here an hour.'

He wound in his line, scrutinized the hook, eyed the water and the sky, and deliberated. I remained respectfully silent. 'I think,' he eventually announced, 'we'll try a worm.'

The Angler's Mate picked up an Oxo tin, gave it a delicate shake, and extracted a long and lugubrious-looking worm. The Angler took it, examined it approvingly, and threaded it slowly on to his hook. After the first quick

 65

close-up I stared desperately into the middle distance, while my breakfast hovered menacingly in my throat.

'Not the weather for tench,' said the Angler as he swung the worm through the air and plunged it into the lake. 'We'll try for rudd.'

For the next hour or so we tried for rudd. Worm after worm was taken from the Oxo tin, attached to the hook and consigned to the deep. But the rudd apparently found them even less attractive than I did. At about six o'clock the Angler showed the first sign of impatience. He actually sighed. 'Not very good sport this morning,' he said. I, with some difficulty, said nothing.

A swan cruised smoothly across the lake, looked at the bedraggled trio on the bank, gave a scornful croak and cruised smoothly away again. It was the first indication that the lake contained any form of life at all. I felt slightly heartened.

At half-past six the Angler wound in his line for the umpteenth time. For the umpteenth time I had the wild hope that he had decided he had had enough. And for the umpteenth time I found I had under-estimated him. 'We will try,' he said, 'a float.'

A sliver of wood, its bright colours looking positively garish in the sombre light of early morning, joined forces with the latest worm and floated peacefully on the water. Three pairs of eyes watched it intently. Even the swan came back to study it. Just before seven o'clock it up-ended, twitched and disappeared.

Immediately our still life group sprang into action. The Angler flipped his rod and took the strain. The Angler's Mate seized a long-handled net and poised himself at the water's edge. I fluttered anxiously between the two, whispering encouragement. The swan, quite carried away by all this, flapped two enormous wings.

A dirty-brown fish appeared at the surface. The Angler's Mate scooped it up in his net, and all four of us gazed at it admiringly. 'A splendid rudd,' I ventured. 'As a matter of fact,' said the Angler, 'it's a tench.' 'But I thought you were fishing for rudd!' I exclaimed. 'It's a great sport,' said the Angler. 'Never know what's going to happen next.'

The tench weighed about a pound and a half. It lay in the net, twitching spasmodically and eyeing us balefully. As the climax of two hours' chilly fishing, it could have been more impressive, but it was a fish and we had caught it. Oddly enough, ten minutes later we caught another, and twenty minutes after that the Angler hauled in a pike – a small one, admittedly, but

nevertheless a pike, the famed freshwater shark. Things were moving with almost unnerving speed.

At a quarter to eight the Angler decided to call it a day. 'You must come again,' he said. Memories of that cursed alarm, of the indigestible breakfast, of the battle with the car engine, of the hours of inactivity, had already faded. I could only think of the excitement of landing those two tench and the pike. 'Yes,' I said, 'I really must.'

Back home the Little Woman yawned as I told her about our seven tench and our four enormous pike. 'How big were the tench?' she asked. 'Oh, about four or five pounds,' I said casually. 'But you should have seen the one that got away.'

It's a Boy

For the second time in a fortnight, following that experiment with early morning angling, I was out of bed and facing a darkened world, but this time we were after a bigger catch. It was soon after four o'clock when I woke. 'I think,' said the Little Woman, 'you had better phone for the nurse . . .'

I had read so much
on the subject by this time that the
subsequent routine came almost automatically.
I went to the kitchen, lined up an imposing
array of jugs and basins, and put on the kettle. Boiling
water, I knew, was almost more vital on these occasions than the
Little Woman herself. Soon I was surrounded by cauldrons
of bubbling, steaming, well-and-truly-boiling water. Several hours later, of
course, when it had long since cooled, I threw the whole lot away.

Meanwhile came the nurse, the doctor, and expulsion from the upper floor.
Down in my sauna-bath of a kitchen, with the Pooch panting heavily in one
corner and the cat turning purple in another, and darkness cloaking the world
outside the steamed-up windows, I nerved myself for the inevitable hours of
vigil. That was when I discovered I had just one cigarette.

It is moments such as this, I imagine, when people start throwing crockery.
They laugh maniacal laughs and gibber ghastly gibberish. In extreme cases
they may even give up smoking. I am proud to record that my reaction was

limited to a few brief comments to the Pooch. The comments were quite colourful, and the Pooch has never quite looked me in the eye since, but on the whole my restraint was remarkable. I put the cigarette on the table, I sat down quietly, and I looked at it. The time was five o'clock.

To the best of my knowledge there was a nearby newsagent and tobacconist who opened at seven. To be scientific and methodical I proposed to light that cigarette on the stroke of six.

At ten past five I stubbed out the dog-end. It had tasted, oddly enough, like decaying fish. It was all of ten minutes before I felt like having another smoke. And from that point until the magic hour of seven, life became something of a blur.

I can remember making a great many pots of tea, most of which went down the sink. I can remember pacing around the lawn in the darkness with the Pooch in close attendance, giving me strange sidelong glances. At one point I believe I was seriously contemplating the possibility of beating on my neighbour's front door and offering him fabulous sums for his stock of tobacco. But when I suggested this plan to the Pooch he looked so appalled I had to drop it.

There was one terrible moment when the paper-boy came. The unsuspecting youth entered the front gate, whistling some cheery air and blissfully at peace with the world, while I crouched in the kitchen, peering through a crack in the curtains at his fingers in search of a tell-tale yellow stain. As he pushed the paper through the letterbox I flung open the door. It must have been a nasty moment; in all the months he has delivered papers to us the house has been silent as a tomb. We had never even seen each other before. Now he was confronted by a wild-eyed apparition. He took it remarkably well.

'Good morning,' he said.

'Good morning,' I said. 'Do you smoke?'

I never found out. At this point the Pooch appeared from behind me and prepared to leap up and lick the lad's face. I knew his intention but of course the unfortunate lad did not. He had never met the Pooch before either, and could easily have assumed that his life was in danger. The sight of the two of us, both slavering gently, was too much. He retreated at considerable speed to his bicycle, and I have not seen him since.

I believe the postman arrived soon afterwards, and being a postman of some experience was probably made of sterner stuff, but I had not the heart to find out. I concentrated instead on reading the paper. It was only when I

had read every item except the Situations Wanted and the Sales by Auction that a great truth dawned upon me. If the newspaper had been delivered, the newsagent must be open. As I dashed for the door, the clock was just striking seven.

The man in the shop was most considerate. My money was cached in the unapproachable upstairs, but I threw myself on his mercy and he gave me a packet on tick. I nearly finished them in the next hour, but by then it was all over. And although the situation is unlikely to arise again in the immediate future, I shall always keep twenty tucked away in the sideboard just in case. Another couple of hours like that and the Pooch will cut me dead.

Oh yes. It's a boy. And he's a non-smoker.

(For the record: I gave up cigarettes myself a couple of years later).

Early morning guide to newspapers and who reads what:

The Times is read by people who run the country.

The *Mirror* is read by people who think they run the country.

The *Guardian* is read by the people who think they ought to run the country.

The *Morning Star* is read by people who think the country ought to be run by another country.

The *Daily Mail* is read by the wives of the people who run the country.

The *Financial Times* is read by the people who own the country.

The *Daily Express* is read by the people who think the country ought to be run as it used to be.

The *Daily Telegraph* is read by the people who still think it is.

The *Sun* and the *Star* are read by the people who don't care who runs the country so long as she's got a big bust.

9

Early Morning
Preoccupations

The early morning may not seem the ideal time to become preoccupied with anything except whether the hot water is hot enough, the eggs are cooked firmly enough, or the children are off to school promptly enough. But in spite of these routine problems, or perhaps because of them, many people relish having something else to think about at breakfast-time, not too taxing but perhaps a little provoking, entirely divorced from the day-to-day hassle of getting up, getting dressed, getting a bite, and getting going.

The press and the broadcasters are only too happy to supply an appropriately trivial topic. Sometimes they do it intentionally, when perhaps a challenge is issued for the most outrageous shop title (can it be true that in Alexandria, Virginia, there is a carpet stall in the market bearing the legend 'Alexandria's Rugtime Stand'?). Often it is accidental, when a mispronounced place name on the radio or a foolish phrase in the paper sets the adrenalin flowing and the telephone ringing.

There is nothing new in all this. I have before me a cutting from an eighty-year-old newspaper which had obviously invited its readers to send in quaint quotes from parental 'Sorry little Johnnie missed school' letters. Some may seem a little dated: 'Please excuse Harry. He addent no trousers and es

 71

father wouddent let him come without any'; or 'Jane has had to stop at home as I have had twins. It shant occur again.' Others seem quite typical: 'I must strictly forbid you to punish Thos again for anything he does, as we never do so ourselves except in self-defence.' All of them could be guaranteed to take the eye of the early morning reader and probably provoke more contributions.

Here are some of the more recent topics which have captured attention in the early morning before normal work begins: genuinely pre-occupational preoccupations.

Words for The Eating

Lexicography and breakfast hardly seem to go together, but early morning listeners and readers do get very worked up over words – their correct use, their correct spelling in the papers, their correct pronunciation on the air. Spelling is full of pitfalls in a language where the same sound can be written down so many ways. (It might have occurred with every third word heard – who could help being deterred? It's absurd . . .) And while the BBC Pronunciation Unit – who get very irritated if you call them the Pronounciation Unit – do their best to keep us on the straight and narrow, in the hurly-burly of 'live' current affairs broadcasting we can slip up, and then it is the listeners who put us right.

Place names are probably the biggest hazard. Only a Norfolkman, for instance, would know without checking that Wymondham is pronounced Windum, Happisburgh is Hazebro, and Costessey is reduced to Cossy. But the real problems arise when not even the locals can agree. Taking Norfolk examples again, Hunstanton can be Hunston to the local gentry, while Stiffkey can be Stewky to the local cockler. Further afield, should Cirencester be Cicester or Cister? If not, why call Bicester Bister? And once we cross the Channel, logic completely deserts us. If we say Lee-on for Lyons and Marsay for Marseilles, why on earth should we not say Paree?

The Welsh, incidentally, have provided some terrifying tongue-twisters for the unwary broadcaster. One can not only trip over a Llan-mine; even an innocent little name like Dyfed can be booby-trapped. I came upon it unexpectedly in a weather forecast, and took it at face value. A Welsh listener called Ruth Cole sent me this rather charming rebuke:

 73

Surprised, I said 'Heavens above-ed!
Is that where I liv-ed and lov-ed?'
When the Preselis in Wales
Are threatened by gales,
Remember: not 'Diff-ed' but 'Dove-ed'.

There is some excuse for mispronouncing names if there has been no chance to check, and sometimes we can even put up a case for apparently mispronouncing ordinary English words. There is a frequently recurring early morning controversy, for instance, over 'controversy'. When I joined the BBC I had always said 'con*trov*ersy' with the accent on the second syllable. According to the Pronunciation Unit at that time it had to be '*cont*roversy'. I dutifully trained myself to say it that way, with the accent on the first syllable – only to find a few years later that the rules had eased and either version was acceptable. Unfortunately not every listener agrees; the arguments still continue.

Similarly there is less rigidity now about the way words are used. For months in the early mornings I fought a rearguard action against the use of 'hopefully' to mean 'I hope', as in 'Hopefully I shall be in time for a drink.' I maintained that 'hopefully' meant 'full of hope', as in 'Hopefully I looked at the barman.' Alas, the forces of reason collapsed around me and scattered in unseemly retreat. They argued that it had become 'common usage' and was therefore now acceptable. In the same way sentences can now end unblushingly with prepositions, and infinitives can be split without quarter.

In this sort of climate, small wonder that old friends like Fahrenheit have been replaced first by Centigrade, then by Celsius – but not without a struggle. Mr G. L. Leigh of West London sent me the correspondence he had had with the Deputy Principal Meteorological Officer at the London Weather Centre, in a period when many other listeners were complaining over their breakfast tables every time the weathermen used this unfamiliar word.

In response to his rather brusque request for an explanation – 'What is the philosophy behind the sudden usage of this wierd neologism?' – the DPMO patiently replied:

'The word is in fact the name of the French gentleman who invented this particular scale of temperature. It has replaced Centigrade, as the word Centigrade is a generic term applied to any scale with 100 gradations . . .'

Mr Leigh was not to be placated: 'We have now got to put up with a foreign name that hardly anyone will be able to spell properly,' he snapped back. He

74

then observed that according to the Oxford English Dictionary Supplement, Celsius was not French but Swedish. Having slipped that one past the DPMO's guard, he followed up with, in my view, a technical knockout: 'What if this scale of temperature had been invented,' he asked, 'by a Monsieur Avant-Garde-Zoute-Alors-Merde?'

Alas, we have yet to revert to Centigrade, but there are other battles still to be fought, and our early morning listeners are in there fighting. We still get a violent reaction, and rightly so, when someone referring to a ten-year period calls it a 'decayed'. And I am entirely behind a Mr Sidney Scott of Watford who wrote to me deploring the use of 'billion' to mean a thousand million. Lest you fall into the trap yourself, here is his argument:

'For the prefix ''bi'' we can see that two millions are combined, and they are combined by multiplication. Moreover we cannot object that we need a word for a thousand million because we have always had one. Here is the correct table:

One million	: 1,000,000
One milliard	: 1,000,000,000
One billion	: 1,000,000,000,000.'

It is the Americans (of course) who are to blame for the bogus billion, but not for everything. The same Mr Scott reprimanded the chairman of ICI for an early morning use of 'criteria' as a single noun, and an MP for referring to hooligans indulging in 'animal behaviour' – animals, said Mr Scott, behaved far better than hooligans and should not be insulted in this way.

Happily such criticisms are not aimed solely at the broadcasters. Mr David Rowe complained in *The Times* one morning about the use of the abbreviation 'K' to represent thousands of pounds. 'Quite apart from being inelegant,' he wrote, 'the term does not even have the advantage of brevity. The user takes up just as much time, after saying something is to cost so many K, with a pause for dramatic effect.' He did note, however, that *The Times* remained good value at £0.00023K.

In the same columns an advertiser came under fire from a Mr Tim Barraclough for claiming that a certain garden trolley would enable its purchaser to 'kiss your aching back goodbye'. 'Sir,' wrote Mr Barraclough, 'when I can perform this feat, I will buy the trolley.' The advertiser, also a student of words and their meanings, came back with this reply: 'Assuming the surname Barraclough derives from ''Barrow: a hill'' and ''Clough: a ravine'', the gentle-

man may need help in moving heavy loads. We have therefore sent him a trolley with our compliments . . .

It was about that time that Philip Howard, the regular *Times* contributor, treated his early morning readers to a swift excursion around the quirks and quiddities of the language ('Quiddities In' the sub-editor headed it, to his lasting shame). Mr Howard demonstrated how words can have two quite opposite meanings: 'to cleave', for instance, can mean to cling together and to split apart; 'fast' can mean speedy, and stationary; 'downs' can actually be quite high up.

The section from his article I commended to our early morning listeners was his Unhelpful Alphabet. A for Aegis, B for Bdellium, C for Ctenoid, D for Djinn, and so on. For J he had Jipijapa (pronounced hipihapa), though for old times' sake, from the ho-ho days, I wish he had chosen jojoba. After M for Mnemonic he had N for Misprint; yes, it *was* a joke. And so on. Some letters were unaccounted for, and I exhorted our listeners to supply them. I got no response; I hope he fared better.

One final thought on the present-day use and misuse of words originated in a New York weekly, was reproduced one morning in the *Daily Mail* and was forthwith quoted by me. It might be called 'The Bum's Lament':

'I used to think I was poor. Then they told me I wasn't poor, I was needy. Then they told me it was self-defeating to think of myself as needy; I was deprived. Then they told me I was really under-privileged, but under-privileged was over-used, so actually I was disadvantaged.

'I still don't have a dime. But I have a great vocabulary.'

Anything You Can Do . . .

Everyone loves to claim a record. Everyone else, as soon as it is mentioned in the early morning, loves to cap it. Ever since the first rural cleric (or was it a retired schoolteacher?) claimed to have heard the first cuckoo, the correspondence columns of the newspapers and of the air have been bombarded with claims and counter-claims regarding all manner of unlikely achievements. Sometimes they reach *Guinness Book of Records* proportions; early-morning readers are put off their breakfast by tales of high-speed egg-eating or in-credible feats with jellied eels.

But at that time of day, whimsy is preferable to gluttony. A pleasant example

 76

came from a resident
of St George's Square SW1,
who wrote:
'The council relaid the road
yesterday afternoon in
St George's Square.
At 7.30 a.m. this morning
the Gas Board started
to dig it up. Is this a new
world record?'
The challenge produced
no other contenders, only a letter
from the Gas Board, saying
the piece of road they dug
up had been underneath the
council's parked steamroller,
the weight of which had fractured
their main. This very reasonable
explanation must have discouraged any further jibes at the
nationalized industries – at least for
that week.

There was plenty of reaction however
from *Today* listeners when Mr Eric
Cochran, an expatriate working in San Cataldo on the extreme
southern heel of Italy, told us he
could hear the programme each
morning by parking on the top floor
of a multi-storey car park and
erecting a king-size car aerial. He
carried out this exercise every day
on his way to work, and we marvelled

that he had not been arrested as some sort of spy. We also foolhardily observed that, as he was some 1250 miles from Radio 4's main transmitter at Droitwich, he might be our furthest-flung listener. The suggestion was soon flung back.

Almost immediately we had a phone call from a listener who was tuned into us in Torremolinos, which she claimed was 1300 miles away. She knew that, she said, because her husband had once cycled there. It seems, however, he must have taken a devious route, because a Navy man consulted his computer and phoned us to say that Malaga, the nearest the computer could get to Torremolinos, was only 922.7 miles away. He also checked on calls we had from Tangiers (959.8 miles) and Iceland (988.7).

So for twenty-four hours Mr Cochran retained the title. But in a couple of days more contestants had thrown their radios into the ring. Mr Len Hunt remembered hearing the programme in an Algerian desert township called Ouargla (I hope he enjoyed our weather forecasts). Mr Robert F. Hodgson regularly listened to the programme during a holiday in Lanzarote in the Canary Islands, some 1700 miles from London as the package tour flies.

We disallowed a bid from a British Airways pilot who told us he tuned in his automatic direction finder to the Daventry transmitter when he was still over Newfoundland, 2500 miles away. But we could not argue with a Captain Long of Sevenoaks, who told us that when he was in Yokohama in Japan in the 1960s he could tune in to what was then the Light Programme. He said he wrote to the BBC about it, and was told – rather loftily, no doubt – that this was nothing unusual.

So we checked with our Engineering Information Service, which of course we should have done in the first place but it would rather have spoilt the fun. Sure enough, they confirmed that given certain freak weather conditions, *Today* could be picked up almost anywhere. We therefore had a potential listening audience of – yes, milliards. Is this a . . . Sorry!

The Game of The Name

One early morning frivolity has survived in newspapers and radio programmes perhaps longer than any other. The name of this game is names, and the bizarre juxtapositions that can be achieved by marriage, by business partnerships, even by naïve parents. It must be over ten years ago that I first quoted

the firm of solicitors in County Sligo called Argue and Phibbs, and similar contributions have been pouring in ever since.

A recent flurry, which spread through much of the national press as well as on the air, began, I believe, with a member of Cheshire Golf Club pointing out that his fellow members included Mr Bird, Mr Duck, Mr Swan, Miss Quail, Miss Martin, Mr Swift, Mr Peacock and Mr Swallow. His own name was Partridge.

This prompted the Royal Parks Department to report that on its London staff were Messrs Fox, Hare, Sparrow, Hart, Hunter and – last – Straw. A Malayan customs officer claimed he had three colleagues called Fish, Rice and Curry. And a Squadron Leader Butcher recalled he was at school with a Baker and – no, just a Tallow.

At Bournemouth Grammar School in 1937 there were three boys in the same class called Carr, Laurie and Buss. In No. 3 Company, 2nd Battalion, Coldstream Guards there were Guardsman Lock, Corporal Stock and Guardsman Barrell. At the Canadian High Commission in London there were simultaneously a Scott and an Amundsen. A Wembley dentist claimed he had made successive appointments for a Mr Cumming, Mrs Gowing and Miss Wendt, while in similar vein a trio of cadets who joined the Colonial Service in the days of Northern Rhodesia were called Tooke, Short and Going. To complete that theme, Toc H in the 1940s had a Mr Bean, a Rev Gawne and a Mr Dunnett.

At the Treasury an official called Chorley had two assistants called Miss Arndts and Mr Clapp. They were known collectively as Clapp, Arndts, here comes Chorley. Two time-conscious fitters in the test sheds at Rolls Royce's Hucknall works were called Arthur Noon and Arthur Minitt. And an RAF rigger who reversed the trim tab control cables on a plane, thus making it near-lethal, turned out to be Rigger Mortis.

There were some nice little individual offerings. In Cerne Abbas in Dorset Canon Liddell-Payne lived in Piddle Lane, while a door-to-door salesman for the Easifit stretch cover company was called Paul de Bell. Did he have a colleague, one wonders, called Paul de Other-One?

The most embarrassing combinations seem to be intentionally self-inflicted. Why else should a girl called Molly marry a man called Coddle? Why did a Miss Rose, who had been christened Wild by her romantically inclined parents, fail to seek pastures new through matrimony, and instead marry a Mr Bull? Should a Mr Screech have taken up dentistry? And how could a Mr Jerry

Bilder of Stanmore, having suffered such a blow from his parents, decide to go into housing development?

Business partnerships are less able to pick and choose, though it may have occurred to the insurance broking firms of C. E. Heath and Hogg Robinson, when they decided not to merge, that they had avoided becoming Heath Robinson. Others have not been put off. Thus a printing firm in Belfast acquired the title Reid and Wright, and in Nottingham there are the building contractors Bodgitt and Scarper. Then, sure enough, someone wrote in to say there was a solicitors' firm in County Sligo called Argue and Phibbs. After ten years, we had gone full circle.

Come to The Bizarre

Apart from names, anything with a flavour of the bizarre seems to be particularly savoured at breakfast time, whether it be a news story or indeed a non-news story. The *Guardian*, for instance, runs a silly season competition for the most inconsequential item of news from a local newspaper – it assumes that such an item would never be found in the *Guardian* itself – offering to the winner the Small Earthquake Challenge Cup, named in honour of that original classic headline: 'Small Earthquake in Chile: Not Many Dead.'

One of the best offerings came from Mr John Colman of Barnet. It was a real gripper from the *Barnet Borough Times*, which I passed on to our early morning listeners: 'From lunchtime on Tuesday last week until 9.26 the following day, a total of twelve millimetres of rain, less than three-quarters of an inch, fell on the Barnet borough. "It was not all that heavy," said a council spokesman.'

Bizarre book titles are always a winner in the early morning. I quoted one or two from a whole book of them which took no chances with its own title; it was just called *Bizarre Books*. I particularly enjoyed the visions conjured up by *Truncheons, Their Romance and Reality*, and *The Inheritance of Hairy Ear Rims*. But the latter is far surpassed in scientific obscureness by some of the titles chosen by students for their PhD theses, which I quoted from *The Times* Diary.

Julie Jackson of Newcastle University set the pace with her *Life History Characteristics of Midges in Temporary Peat Bogs*. A Leicester student came up with *Bees and Beekeeping in Classical Antiquity*, while in London a student concentrated on a more precise aspect, *The Leg Muscles of the Adult Honey-Bee*.

 80

From a rather
different field came the
bewildering *Melopoeia,*
Phonopoeia, Logopoeia and
the Evolution of Ezra Pound's
Literary Technique; I trust
Mr Pound's technique was
less convoluted than
that of his chronicler.

An Oxford student came up with the rather charming topic, *The Gnome and Its Use in Certain Old English Poems,* which must have run to all of half a page. My personal award for the most unlikely title, let alone the most longwinded, went to a Belfast student for *The Influence On Their Decision Making Of The Different Interpretations of Actors Involved in the Garbage Strike and Boycott of 1968 in Memphis, Tennessee.* Even if it never existed, full marks for inventing it.

Truth, however, is still stranger than fiction. Who could invent the exploit of four limbless ex-servicemen, all of whom had lost both legs, who went on a New Beaujolais race in reverse, taking the first English wine of the season to France under the slogan: 'You don't have to be legless to enjoy English wine.' Who would credit that a great many gullible New Yorkers contributed quite happily to a 'charity' calling itself the Fund for the Widow of the Unknown Warrior? And who could devise a police report quite as preposterous as this offering from the *Chichester Observer*:

'An elderly motorist given the standard eyesight test from sixty-seven feet by Sussex police after an accident could not even see the vehicle. He could

 81

only read the numberplate when he was eighteen inches from the rear of the vehicle and leaning slightly forward. He was registered as partially sighted, and usually drove with an elderly passenger who helped him by telling him what else was on the road and in which direction to steer . . .'

The early morning item which we particularly cherished in this bracket was the offer of an enterprising undertaker (in the United States, of course) to arrange for the ashes of the deceased to be scattered in space. Mr A. G. Causer of Wolverhampton, much taken with this proposal, penned a poem over his porridge, which in due course I recited. The demand for copies – particularly from old folks' homes – was quite remarkable.

> If you're feeling none too agile, or particularly fragile,
> And you think the time has come to make your will,
> Those unseemly family clashes over where to bung your ashes
> May be ended by a simple codicil.
>
> The progress made by science means that undertakers' clients
> Can now be soon despatched to outer space.
> Before the mourners can absorb it, you'll be blasted into orbit
> To occupy your final resting place.
> Let your old pals see their friend off in a pyrotechnic send-off
> But don't leave the arrangements just to chance.
> For your friendly undertaker gets you closer to your Maker
> If you make your reservation in advance.
>
> This radical proposal for celestial disposal
> Has only one grave drawback I can see.
> If the funerary missile is suspected to be fissile,
> Then it could provoke the start of World War Three.

There Goes Another Postilion

Ever since someone discovered in an English–French phrasebook the despairing cry, 'Help! My postilion has been struck by lightning!' there has been a market for The Phrase You Are Least Likely to Need On A Foreign Holiday. It was given a new impetus when readers of *The Times* opened their newspaper one July morning in 1985 and read a delightful article by Miles Kington based on the advice he had read in a travel book. 'It is said that an effective and

enjoyable way of improving your fluency is to read the local comic strip magazines.'

Miles duly did so, and came up with such valuable contributions to international understanding as 'I am a Venusian policeman and you are under arrest, earthling.' But what started as a joke soon developed into an exchange of genuine phrasebook treasures which lasted for many mornings to come. Some of them proved even more outlandish than the strip cartoons.

Jean Buckley of West Norwood was the first to follow up the Kington article. It recalled for her a phrasebook she discovered on her first visit to Finland in 1961. Its prime offering demonstrated the innate courtesy of the average Finn,

even under trying circumstances: 'Excuse me, I hate to trouble you, but your motorcycle is standing on my foot.'

Two days later the issue was broadened by two of my BBC colleagues, Libby Purves and Paul Heiney, whose joint interest in sailing had led them to a book called *Universal Yacht Signals* published in the 1890s. It included signals requesting the shore station to prepare a vapour bath for the incoming yachtsman, and also to supply marmalade, 'orange unless specified'. In return

 84

the shore signaller could offer helpful advice to the new arrival with Hoist 6419, which reads 'I can strongly recommend my washerwoman.'

After this maritime diversion the correspondence was brought back on course by Sir William Hayter, former British Ambassador to Moscow. When he was appointed the Foreign Office provided him with a tutor to help him brush up his Russian. 'Two of the sentences he selected for me stick in my memory, though I never found much use for them in Moscow,' Sir William wrote. 'One was: "Near the house there is a small dark park." The other was: "Hurrah! The Cossacks are attacking again!"'

Peggy Visick of Truro quoted an Italian phrasebook which prepared her for the worst with the enquiry: 'Which way did the tanks go?' Lady Maddocks found a useful opening gambit in her Portugese phrasebook: 'Have you read much Sheridan lately?' She also recalled learning Swahili from a grammar written in 1875, which contained guidance on the correct way of saying in Swahili: 'The angry European has killed the wicked cook.'

That may seem a little dated, but how much further away seems this offering from Dr W. Alan Heaton-Ward of Clifton. Shortly after the last war he came across a booklet of useful phrases for Danes visiting England which included: 'Yorkshire won the county cricket championship last season.' The suggested follow-up is marginally more topical: 'Yes, but Surrey ran them very close.'

Mrs Priscilla Mitchell of Totnes relished the memory of a phrasebook she borrowed for a visit to Yugoslavia in 1954 which contained the handy throwaway line, 'My father has an airship.' This, she said, caused considerable delight among some members of the Yugoslav Air Force who were sharing her journey. Another visitor to Eastern Europe, Alec Rose of Hockley, remembered a Czech phrasebook containing the modest announcement, 'I am a Hero of the Soviet Union.' The book was of course pre-1968.

Mrs Sheila Vince of Coventry brought an Oriental flavour to the discussion, with her recollection that as a student physiotherapist she once helped a seriously ill Chinese patient to get out of bed. The patient's phrasebook was no great help in conducting this manoeuvre. The only entries remotely connected with hospital care were 'I am sorry that your concubine is sick' and 'Here comes the executioner.'

But not even the most assiduous phrasebook compiler can be expected to cover every eventuality. For example, the Rev R. Meredith wrote that at an ecumenical centre in France he found himself in urgent and embarrassed need of a Dutch phrase which the average traveller might have managed without.

Something on the lines of 'Madam, I think your bath is overflowing. There is a damp patch on my ceiling.'

But they do their best. Surely the first prize for inconsequential information must go to the entry in a Dutch–English phrasebook which another cleric, the Rev David Copley of Halesowen, came upon in a Japanese prisoner-of-war camp during the Second World War. It had been left behind in a bungalow where he was temporarily housed. 'The price of an egg,' it revealed, 'is half the cost of ringing up the vicar.'

Finally Baroness Twickel quoted an occasion when one of these apparently useless phrases looked like coming into its own. An aunt of hers learned French from a lesson book which contained a picture of a broken-down covered waggon, and bore the text: 'Est-ill arrivé un accident au chariot?' Years later she was involved in a road accident in France and was convinced that at last the moment for demonstrating her linguistic prowess had come. She approached the distraught driver and enquired elegantly if his covered wagon had broken down. His reply was never recorded.

The Writing on The Wall

Notices in public places, whether they are erected officially or scrawled on a wall, can offer some delightful breakfast-time material, so long as the graffiti is selected with care. There was a long-running discussion on eccentric signs in one morning paper (in this case, not signs of *The Times* but signs of the *Daily Telegraph*) from which I was able to extract some acceptable offerings.

It started with an old favourite, this time sighted in Yorkshire, which said simply: 'Do not throw stones at this sign.' On similar lines was a contribution from Bexhill: 'Please do not lean cycles against this sign.' A sign in Carlisle just said: 'Not to be removed,' and on the Isle of Wight was a particularly enterprising effort, a sign which appeared to be gibberish until looked at through a mirror, when it read: 'Thank you for looking at me through a mirror.'

If further proof were needed that signwriters have souls, there was a sign in Dartford which said engagingly, 'Please ignore this sign.' Not intentionally teasing, perhaps, was the board a lady hiker discovered on top of a lonely tor in Dartmoor which requested 'Queue here.' But there must surely have been a tongue-filled cheek when a massive boulder weighing several tons, beside

 86

the road at Glenshee in Tayside, was inscribed with the warning, 'Not to be taken away.'

The gleam may be in the eye of the signwriter or in the mind of the signreader. On the road from Bournemouth to Ringwood, for example, there is a venerable sign belonging to the Laing Construction Company, indicating some long-deserted site. It took the devious mind of a Mr Walker of Bournemouth to conclude that this was probably the original Auld Laing Sign.

Somewhere on the borderline between official notices and graffiti must be the message pinned to a church notice board in Manchester: 'Re power failure. The Electricity Board engineer called and has lightened your darkness.'

In the field of genuine graffiti there seems to be less inventiveness these days. Old favourites like 'Apathy Rules – Who Cares?' or 'Love Thy Neighbour – But Don't Get Caught' seem to come round all too often. Individualistic talents seem to have been blotted out in the Age of the Aerosol Spray. So I seized upon a piece of creative writing which may give hope of a better class of graffiti taking over our walls. It actually appeared on a railway station in Manhattan, but as we import most American idiosyncrasies we may well see its like in due course around Euston or King's Cross.

'X times N (to the Nth) plus Sin Y times N (to the Nth) equals Sin Z times N (to the Nth), has no solution for integer values of X, Y and Z when N is greater than 2. I have discovered a truly remarkable proof of this, but I can't write it now because my train is coming.'

The Older They Come, The Younger They Feel

There are few times of day when you feel your age more than in the early morning, so it is not surprising that the subject of growing old should catch on over the breakfast table. How do you define old age? And how do you know when you have reached it? It surely cannot be when policemen start looking too young, because I cannot recall a time when they haven't. I find it far more salutary when I discover that those venerable old fogies quavering away in front of the blackboard in my schooldays were in fact much younger then than I am now; while their present-day successors I find difficult to distinguish from their pupils.

This morose meditation was brought on one morning when I read a *Times* letter from Sir Antony Part. He had been mulling over the subject too, and at

the age of sixty-nine had slightly more reason to do so than I had. But he had come to a more heartening conclusion. He had decided that old age should be defined as ten years older than he was, at any given time. He had held that view since he was twenty and saw no reason to alter it now he was approaching seventy. He hoped never to overtake that senile decade.

Subsequent correspondents confessed, however, that old age had overtaken them, and they could pinpoint precisely when that knowledge dawned upon them. For instance, there was the retired headmaster who said the first time he really felt old was when he was queuing for his pension and found himself behind a former pupil who was queuing for his!

Robert Hodd of Blackpool quoted an experience that many of us must have shared. It is not the first time a small boy calls you Sir, though that can be chastening enough. It is when a young man offers his seat, apparently to the young lady you are standing next to, and then says: 'No, not for her, sir. It's for you.' My own most ignominious moment came when I went to a hotel to collect the twenty-five-year-old daughter of a friend of mine, a most attractive girl. As she came down the stairs towards me, every head in the foyer turned. The women were envying her, the men without doubt were envying me.

The fact that I had a case with me (full of business papers, but they were not to know that) added a little extra spice to the situation. I looked forward to the gratifying moment when she would greet me, perhaps exchange a kiss or a hug, and walk with me arm-in-arm to the door.

It was not to be. In a voice which carried to every straining ear she cried: 'Hallo, Uncle. Let me carry your bag.'

The Question's an Orange

Perhaps it was St Paul who started it with all those epistles to his extensive mailing list of Ephesians, Galatians, Corinthians and the like, but present-day clerics do seem to be the most prolific of early morning correspondents, hoping maybe to achieve the same literary immortality, or at least become a collected works and go into paperback. They will pontificate on the most unecclesiastical of topics, and none could have been more inconsequential, yet highly contro-versial, than that chosen by the Rev E. J. Elwin of Bradford Peverell in Dorset.

The good Mr Elwin was greatly exercised over the different methods that could be employed to eat an orange. He listed no fewer than ten different approaches. They ranged from making a small hole in the orange and sucking out the juice (a singularly wasteful procedure) to cutting it into pyramid-shaped segments and biting the flesh off the rind. He seemed to cover all the exotic alternatives to the traditional form of attack, removing the peel and splitting the orange into its natural segments. But there was more orange-lore to come.

Professor Gareth Morris reminded Mr Elwin that had he held the living of Cranford he would have known that oranges were only to be sucked in the privacy of one's own room. A more sensuous technique was employed by Mrs Judy Garland (not the erstwhile associate of the Wizard of Oz, but perhaps a wizard of the orange). She recalled that as a child she rolled the fruit on the carpet, exerting a gentle pressure with the ball of her foot until it was soft. A small circle of rind was then cut off at the top and a lump of sugar inserted. 'More pressure on the orange by eager hands until the sugar lump dissolved, then some strong sucks until the orange ran dry!'

This routine was also practised by another clerical contributor, Canon T. Hart of Durham, except that after the rolling process he cut the orange into

four, removing the now loosened peel. 'This method can even be carried off in company,' he claimed. 'The difficulties only begin when undue pressure makes the orange squirt all over your hostess's carpet.'

By now the Great Orange Debate was in full cry over the nation's breakfast tables, with the sight of the marmalade pot as a reminder. Rosemary Underhill of Redhill advocated leaving the rind in place: 'Simply slice thinly and enjoy.' C. R. Lear of Reading cut his oranges in half equatorially and ate them with a teaspoon like a grapefruit, 'the only civilised technique available.' But the clearest and most comprehensive instructions came from Mrs Jacqueline Worthington of Stanstead:

'The simplest and most elegant way to eat an orange is the French method,' she wrote. 'With a dessert knife and fork you cut the unpeeled fruit into quarters and then into eighths. Holding down each segment with the fork, you then neatly cut the flesh from the rind, pick it up on the fork, and eat. This way no juice gets splattered about, there is no messy pulp to deal with, and nothing is wasted.'

If she had not revealed its French connection this approach might have caught on, but what self-respecting Brit is going to emulate the Continentals? I have yet to see an orange tackled in this meticulous fashion. Most of us, I suspect, still grapple with the wretched things with our bare hands.

There is however a device in existence which I can personally commend. It looks like a plastic crochet hook and I believe it used to be given away free at Tupperware parties. The hook cuts the peel to just the right depth, unlike a knife which, if wielded too clumsily, can cause incisions in the segments beneath. Two longitudinal strokes with the hook at right angles, and the quartered peel can be effortlessly removed.

The hazards you encounter next, however, require further expertise. There may be an excess of pith, the segments may refuse to part, you may find a positive plethora of pips. Only a clergyman could do justice to the range of problems thus created, and the solutions available. I am sure we shall not be disappointed.

Farewell to The Ho-Ho

Finally, a respectful genuflection to that early morning preoccupation I became so involved in for a decade or more on the *Today* programme, the ho-ho. We

have long since tried to drop the expression, but letters still come in with clippings and anecdotes and photographs, all claiming a place in the ho-ho saga. It was the way we used to fill a few spare seconds with a little touch of light relief, sometimes so disastrously that in sheer self-defence we groaned 'ho-ho', to show that *we* knew it was awful as well.

You may recall the sort of thing. If there were only a few seconds to spare we might throw in a quick one-liner, like the report from a local paper (*The Enniskillen Impartial Reporter and Farmers' Journal*, it was called, which is a bit of a ho-ho in itself): 'Dr W. T. read an interesting paper on "Idiots from Birth". There were over two hundred present.' Ho-ho . . .

If there were forty-odd seconds to fill, we might venture into something more substantial, like the so-called 'Eurocrat's Dream', said to originate from the headquarters of the EEC: 'Heaven is where the police are British, the cooks are French, the mechanics German, the lovers Italian and it is all organised by the Swiss. Hell is where the chefs are British, the mechanics French, the lovers Swiss, the police German and it is all organised by the Italians.'

There might well be a follow-up the next day, if our listeners were quick off the mark. How about the 'Diplomat's Dream': 'Heaven is an English country house, a Chinese cook, a Japanese wife and an American salary. The nightmare would be a Japanese country house, an English cook, an American wife and a Chinese salary.' Cue for 'ho-ho' . . .

Incidentally the earliest recorded ho-ho, quoted on the *Today* programme in 1972, was a headline from the sports page of the *Daily Telegraph*, hailing a belated first century of the season by a noted county cricketer of the day, Roy Virgin. 'At last,' it declaimed, 'Virgin (121) Gets Share of the Luck!'

We still quote such items but they no longer bear the ho-ho label. Even the catchiest running gag (and it reached the stage where people no longer said hallo to me, they just nudged me and leered 'ho-ho') can develop a limp over the years. We seemed to be reaching the stage where the ho-ho became so-so; we decided to retire it before it became a no-no.

Nevertheless I still treasure my unique collection of ho-ho-bilia. There are all those Christmas cards I receive each year smothered in Yule-tide ho-hos. There are book matches and photographs of Ho-Ho Chinese laundries and restaurants and take-aways, including one from Newcastle-upon-Tyne which serves a dish called Tim-Sum, which I found rather gratifying until I discovered it was a sort of steamed dumpling. It also served something called Fun-Ho,

 91

which I would have enjoyed ordering. ('Let's have some Fun-Ho at the Ho-Ho.' Old habits die hard.).

There are the maps showing far-flung Ho-Hos (including Hho-Hho in Swaziland and Xo-Xo in Mexico, which just about qualify). There are the ho-ho lapel badges, the ho-ho soap, even the ho-ho toilet roll – not forgetting the jojoba shampoo. All these are now just museum pieces, a bizarre bazaar of breakfast-time bygones.

So the ho-ho has gone to join the Heavenly Ho-Host. Yet there are still occasions in the early morning, when a pun has proved particularly appalling, or a crisp exchange has turned soggy, or a pay-off line has failed catastrophically to pay off, and I pause for a moment. And I swear that, somewhere out there, I can hear a disembodied chorus, groaning a sepulchral, lingering 'Ho-Hoooo . . .'

There is no official world champion breakfaster, but if there were, then Peter Dowdeswell of Earls Barton in Northamptonshire must surely be favourite. In the 'Gluttony' section of *The Guinness Book of Records* his name appears more than a dozen times, starting with B for Beer (a yard of ale, 3½ pints, in 6.20 seconds) and ending with S for Strawberries (2½ lbs in 27.19 secs). So far as breakfast fare isconcerned, Mr Dowdeswell has eaten 38 softboiled eggs in 75 seconds (if you prefer them hardboiled it takes a little longer, 14 in 58 seconds, but he has also swallowed 13 raw eggs in a single gulp). He has drunk 2 pints of milk in 3.2 seconds and eaten 144 prunes (which he must have been greatly in need of) in 35 seconds. For American breakfasts he has eaten 62 pancakes, complete with butter and syrup, in just under 7 minutes. In Italy he can cope with 5 lbs of ravioli in 5 minutes 34 seconds (he ate that on the same day as the prunes) or a 100 yards of spaghetti in 21 minutes 7 seconds. Mr Dowdeswell is in his forties; the book does not record his weight.